JAPAN AND THE U.S.

edited by ROBERT EMMET LONG

THE REFERENCE SHELF

Volume 62 Number 2

THE H. W. WILSON COMPANY

New York   1990

THE REFERENCE SHELF

The books in this series contain reprints of articles, excerpts from books, and addresses on current issues and social trends in the United States and other countries. There are six separately bound numbers in each volume, all of which are generally published in the same calendar year. One number is a collection of recent speeches; each of the others is devoted to a single subject and gives background information and discussion from various points of view, concluding with a comprehensive bibliography that contains books and pamphlets and abstracts of additional articles on the subject. Books in the series may be purchased individually or on subscription.

Library of Congress Cataloging-in-Publication Data

Main entry under title:

Japan and the U.S. / edited by Robert Emmet Long.
     p.   cm. — (The Reference shelf ; v. 62, no. 2)
  Includes bibliographical references.
  ISBN 0-8242-0791-2
  1. United States—Foreign economic relations—Japan. 2. Japan-
-Foreign economic relations—United States. 3. United States-
-Commercial policy. 4. Japan—Commercial policy. 5. Corpora-
tions, Japanese—United States. 6. Investments, Japanese—United
States.
  I. Long, Robert Emmet. II. Title: Japan and the US. III. Series.
HF1456.5.J3J365   1990
337.52073—dc20   90-30803
                                                                              CIP

Cover: A portion of the 2,100 Japanese compact car shipment parked at Castle Island, South Boston.
Photo: AP/Wide World Photos

Copyright © 1990 by The H. W. Wilson Company. All rights reserved. No part of this work may be reproduced or copied in any form or by any means, including but not restricted to graphic, electronic, and mechanical—for example, photocopying, recording, taping, or information and retrieval systems—without the express written permission of the publisher, except that a reviewer may quote and a magazine or newspaper may print brief passages as part of a review written specifically for inclusion in that magazine or newspaper.

Printed in the United States of America

CONTENTS

PREFACE 5

I. JAPANESE INVESTMENT IN THE U.S.

Editor's Introduction 7
Janice Castro. I'll Take Manhattan—and Waikiki . Time 8
Marc Beauchamp. Close the Door, They're Coming in
    the Windows .... Forbes 10
Bill Powell. Where the Jobs Are .... Newsweek 12
Love and Hate in America .... The Economist 19

II. AMERICAN COMPANIES IN JAPAN

Editor's Introduction 23
Kathleen K. Wiegner. "A Fine Japanese Company" ......
.... Forbes 24
Barbara Rudolph. Winners against Tough Odds .. Time 28
Joel Dreyfuss. How to Beat the Japanese at Home ......
.... Fortune 30

III. COMPETITION IN THE AUTOMOBILE AND HIGH-TECH
    INDUSTRIES

Editor's Introduction 36
John Merwin. A Tale of Two Worlds .... Forbes 37
James B. Treece. Shaking Up Detroit ... Business Week 43
Eliot Marshall. U.S., Japan Reach Truce in Chips War ..
.... Science 52
George Russell. Trade Face-Off .... Time 56
Bill Powell. Japan Makes the Hit List .... Newsweek 68

IV. THE TRADE WAR CONTROVERSY

Editor's Introduction 72
Bill Powell. The Myths of a Trade War ...... Newsweek   74
John W. Dower. The End of Innocence .... The Nation   78
Richard A. Gephardt. U.S.-Japanese Trade Relations:
    Great Necessities Call Out Great Virtue ....
    .... Vital Speeches of the Day   84
David Halberstam. Of Hubris and Hondas ....
    .... New Perspectives Quarterly   96
Seiichi Kamise. U.S. and Japan Relationship: Economic
    Activities .... Vital Speeches of the Day   101
Lawrence W. Beer. The United States–Japan Partner-
    ship: The Wave of the Present ....
    .... Vital Speeches of the Day   107
William Clark, Jr. U.S.-Japanese Relations in Focus .....
    .... Department of State Bulletin   117
Robert Neff and Paul Magnusson. Rethinking Japan ....
    .... Business Week   125
George R. Packard. The Coming U.S.-Japan Crisis .....
    .... Foreign Affairs   134
Mike Mansfield. The U.S. and Japan: Sharing Our Desti-
    nies .... Foreign Affairs   154

BIBLIOGRAPHY

Books and Pamphlets 168
Additional Periodical Articles with Abstracts 169

PREFACE

The relationship of the U.S. and Japan as trading partners has changed dramatically in the last two decades. Once a junior partner, so to speak, Japan has risen to a position of global importance, challenging the leadership role of the U.S. itself. The shifting nature of the relationship was accelerated during the Reagan years by unprecedented federal deficits occurring in the course of our military buildup. The deficits led to the increased value of the dollar as against the yen, making America less competitive in the world economic market. At the same time the Japanese brought a new efficiency and quality control to the manufacture of goods that earned them huge trade income surpluses. Japan became an "economic Juggernaut," increasingly surpassing its trade rivals in many parts of the globe.

Japan's emergence as a formidable economic power has inevitably disturbed the U.S.-Japan alliance, since Japan's gains have been America's losses. In industry after industry, Japan has gained a larger and larger share of the U.S.'s markets. Nor is this dislocation in the relationship between the countries easily resolved. The U.S. and Japan have different trade philosophies that grow out of their different cultures. Americans are big consumers, less given to saving than spending, while the Japanese are big savers who import much less than they export. They protect their home markets through government restrictions and semi-official business arrangements, and pursue an aggressive policy of staking a large export share in the international marketplace. It has frequently been said that Japan's fiercely competitive drive for supremacy in the marketplace is linked to its nationalism; but this nationalist psychology places Japan at odds with the international balance of trade philosophy of other powers. An accommodation with the internationalist viewpoint would require a change in the whole Japanese way of thinking, which is not likely to come about easily. In the meantime, Japan and the U.S. are drawn to the brink of a trade war that neither side wants and that would be damaging to both.

The first section of this collection is concerned with Japanese direct investment in the U.S. The articles in this section illustrate the love-hate attitude of Americans to the Japanese presence, wounding to national pride but welcome in the capital and the thousands of jobs it provides. Section Two turns to the situation of American companies in Japan that face extremely difficult odds in establishing themselves, but which in a number of cases have had conspicuous success. Section Three deals with the most often discussed areas of U.S.-Japanese competition— automobiles and high-tech industries. It brings out how effectively the Japanese have penetrated the U.S. markets, even on U.S. soil. Section Four focuses upon the mounting friction between the trading partners, the series of U.S. government sanctions against Japan for alleged violations of fair-trade practices, and the new revisionist thinking that seeks to bring the Japanese into more equitable trade arrangements. Articles in this section provide various perspectives on the dispute, which has become an unhealthy strain on the U.S.-Japan alliance.

The editor is indebted to the authors and publishers who have granted permission to reprint the materials in this compilation. Special thanks are due to Joyce Cook and the Fulton Public Library staff, and to the staff of Penfield Library, State University of New York at Oswego.

ROBERT EMMET LONG

February 1990

I. JAPANESE INVESTMENT IN THE U.S.

EDITOR'S INTRODUCTION

Japanese direct investment in the U.S. has been the subject of numerous articles in the press, and in the popular mind has been a source of some concern. It touches the sensitive nerve of national pride, the conviction Americans have of being preeminent in global affairs. The emergence of Japan as a great economic power now "buying up" America itself—its corporate institutions, its real estate and factories—is examined in Section One of this volume. The question is raised as to whether Japanese investment here should be seen as a threat or be viewed welcomingly.

In the first article, Janice Castro in *Time* reports on the sizable Japanese investment in American real estate in the mid-to-late 1980s. As she explains, the depreciation of the dollar against the yen makes it an opportune time for the Japanese to invest, since the yen now buys more. The Japanese have invested extensively in Hawaii, presently owning 9 of the 14 hotels along Waikiki Beach; and they have purchased huge corporate headquarter buildings—landmarks of those cities—in New York, Chicago, and Los Angeles. Moreover, they now own many industrial parks, shopping centers, hotels, and condominiums in many other parts of the country. In a following article in *Forbes*, Marc Beauchamp notes how the Japanese have been building industrial plants in various states, competing with U.S. construction contractors and raising anxieties that the factories they build will use Japanese-made robotics, computers, and machine tools.

In an article in *Newsweek*, Bill Powell discusses the Japanese presence in U.S. industry, particularly in autos and consumer electronics, noting that Japanese concerns employ 250,000 American workers—a figure estimated to rise by another 840,000 in the next decade. For these Americans, who receive highly competitive wages and have good working conditions, the Japanese presence has been welcomed. A final article in *The Economist* considers the "love-hate" attitude of many Americans toward Japanese investment here, but stresses that many of the states are vying for such investment, offering various financial incentives to attract it. It is noted that Japanese direct investment in the U.S. is quite considerable, totaling over $200 billion in 1987—a figure approaching the $250 billion America has invested abroad.

I'LL TAKE MANHATTAN—AND WAIKIKI[1]

Exxon, ABC and Tiffany have more in common than famous names and slick midtown-Manhattan addresses. All have Japanese landlords. Within the past six months, investors from Japan have bought the headquarters buildings of the three firms. In a new twist on the protectionist slogan "Buy American," Japanese firms are literally buying America, or at least choice pieces of it, from New York City high-rises to beachfront hotels in Hawaii. Eager as customers at a close-out sale, these investors from the Far East snapped up as much as $6 billion worth of U.S. real estate last year, more than four times the 1985 level, and they have only begun to shop.

Economic forces on both sides of the Pacific have helped set off this international game of Monopoly. For one thing, Japan's incredible export machine has created a huge pool of excess capital. Japan's trade surplus with the U.S. in 1986 alone was $58.6 billion, and exchange-rate changes over the past two years have sharply boosted Japanese purchasing power in the U.S. The dollar has depreciated in value against the Japanese currency by some 40%, from 260 yen in February 1985 to 153 yen last week. That makes even Manhattan prices seem reasonable. Example: a building that cost $100 million, or 26 billion yen, two years ago would now set back the buyer a relatively paltry 15 billion yen.

Japanese investors are hungry for property because it is very expensive in their own country. The average cost of leasing commercial real estate in Tokyo's saturated downtown market is now more than 20 times as high as it is in New York City, and 30 times as high as in Los Angeles. Meanwhile, the overbuilt American skyline beckons.

[1]Reprint of an article by Janice Castro, *Time* staffwriter. Reprinted by permission from *Time*, V. 129:62. March 9, 1987. Copyright © 1987 Time Inc.

In their invasion of the U.S. property market, the Japanese have spent spectacular sums. Mitsui Real Estate Development paid $610 million for the Exxon Building in Rockefeller Center last December, the highest price ever fetched by a Manhattan office tower. Last November, Daiichi America Real Estate paid an all-time top price for U.S. retail space when it shelled out $94 million, or about $1,000 per square foot, for the Tiffany building on Manhattan's Fifth Avenue. Nissei Realty turned over an estimated $135 million last November for a half share of San Francisco's 38-story Crocker Bank Tower and Galleria shopping center. In December, Sumitomo Life Insurance agreed to pay $145 million, or about $330 per rentable square foot, for an office building under construction in Los Angeles.

Shuwa Investments, a family-owned real estate developer, may be America's largest Japanese landlord. The company made headlines last summer when it bought ARCO Plaza, a prime, 2.4 million-sq.-ft. piece of downtown Los Angeles, for $620 million, in the biggest real estate megadeal in California history. Since September 1985, Shuwa has spent $2 billion to acquire some 12 million sq. ft. of property in the U.S., including two buildings in Century City, Calif., worth $235 million, Chase Plaza in downtown Los Angeles ($103 million) and the ABC tower in Manhattan ($175 million).

While many of the splashiest transactions have involved the purchase of big-city landmarks, Japanese investors have also bought industrial parks, shopping centers, condos and hotels in several states. Nine of the 14 hotels along Waikiki Beach in Hawaii are owned by Japanese landlords. Within a month, Kokusai Jidosha, a real estate company, will close a deal to buy the Hyatt Regency on Maui from Chicago-based VMS Realty for an estimated $319 million.

The Japanese sun is also rising over the U.S. construction industry. Kumagai Gumi, a major Japanese construction firm, started $700 million in Hawaiian projects last year, an enormous sum in a state where all nongovernment construction for 1985 totaled $862 million. Nikko Hotels International is building a 425-room luxury hotel in Chicago's Riverfront Park Development and a 525-room hotel near Union Square in San Francisco. Aoki America Construction is building about 1,000 homes in Raleigh, N.C., in a joint venture with a local investor group.

Some American business managers are pleased with the investment boom. Mike McCormack, a leading commercial-property broker in Honolulu, credits Japanese investments with pulling Hawaii out of a long real estate slump. Since Japanese real estate investors tend to buy for the long haul, many industry experts believe they will make excellent landlords, committed to maintaining the value of their properties. Other U.S. business executives simply view the real estate boomlet as a harmless way to handle America's lopsided balance of payments with Japan by in effect trading high-rises and land for VCRs and cars. After all, the literal translation of *fudosan*, the Japanese word for real estate, is "nonmoving assets." That seems like a fair description of Manhattan skyscrapers.

CLOSE THE DOOR, THEY'RE COMING IN THE WINDOWS[2]

Just what American businessmen need. A new dose of Japanese competition. This time the U.S. construction industry is feeling the heat, and not overseas but right here in the U.S. contractors' own backyard.

Travel up to the Portland, Ore. area. The slump in its wood products businesses has been offset somewhat by Japanese direct investment. Fujitsu America, Inc. is putting up a $30 million magnetic disk plant. Epson, a division of Japan's Hattori Seiko group, is building a $10 million printer assembly plant. Last fall ground was broken for a $260 million semiconductor plant for a joint venture between Sharp and RCA across the Columbia River in Camas, Wash.

But who has the general construction contracts on these plants? Not big U.S. firms like Morrison Knudsen and the Bechtel Group, Inc. but Shimizu America Corp., the local arm of Tokyo's $4.7 billion (1985 sales) Shimizu Construction Co. Ltd., one of Japan's "big five" contractors. Shimizu America was also a prime subcontractor on the Toyota/GM plant in Fremont, Calif. and the Sharp Electronics plant in Memphis, Tenn.

[2]Reprint of an article by Marc Beauchamp, *Forbes* staffwriter. Reprinted by permission of *Forbes* magazine, January 27, 1986. Copyright © Forbes Inc., 1986.

Out in Flat Rock, Mich., Mazda is building its $450 million plant. And Mitsubishi Motors will be breaking ground this spring for a plant in Bloomington, Ill. General contractor on both jobs: the U.S. subsidiary of $4 billion (1985 sales) Kajima Corp., headquartered in Tokyo.

According to Takashi Takemoto, Kajima's New York chief representative, both auto factories will employ "the most advanced automated technology." Takemoto says Kajima is also building a fiber optical communications equipment manufacturing plant for NEC in Portland, which will be finished this year, and a semiconductor plant for Hitachi in Dallas.

Gerald J. Michael, senior consultant with Arthur D. Little, estimates that over the next ten years U.S. companies will spend $100 billion to automate manufacturing facilities. Look for Japanese contracting firms to try for a good-size chunk of this. So far the Japanese builders' clients have mainly been Japanese manufacturers. But they will soon be bidding on U.S. firms' jobs, too.

The rest of Japan's big five contractors—Takenaka, Ohbayashi and Taisei—are also active here. They have been hit with the same falloff in nuclear projects, refineries and OPEC infrastructure that has clobbered Bechtel, Fluor and other U.S. contractors. They are hungry for new business.

"In terms of quality control of brick and mortar, we're going to be challenged," says James (Skip) Law, Hewlett-Packard's corporate manager of land development and planning. H-P recently tied up with builder Bechtel and electronic equipment maker Varian Associates to build automated semiconductor plants. Law says Kajima spends heavily on R&D to provide superior finishes on concrete and tile. Kajima has developed a robot to check for faults. U.S. construction firms, by contrast, spend little on R&D, says Law.

The arrival of the Japanese builders also has disturbing implications for U.S. producers of the hardware and software that go inside the new plants. "The brick and mortar isn't the critical end," says GE's Robert W. Baeder, manager of planning and development. "It's the systems and software." The fear is that, given the chance, Japanese general contractors will likely put Japanese-produced computers, robots and numerically controlled machine tools into the factories they build here, just as U.S. and European contractors often used their own countries' equipment during the OPEC building heyday.

The Japanese are already providing tough competitors in capital equipment. Don Zook, Caterpillar Tractor's assistant director of manufacturing, says Cat "pretty much shops the world for the best stuff at the best price." The Japanese gear, Zook says, "tends to work well the first time." GM, too, imports about half its machine tools, mostly from Japan, and has a joint venture, GMF Robotics, with Japan's Fanuc. The leader in the field, GMF Robotics controls nearly one-third of the U.S. market for robots; around 90% of its products are made in Japan. GMF Robotics is now building a U.S. factory, "for public appearances if nothing else," says a GM spokesman.

Of the $100 billion he thinks U.S. companies will spend to automate, Arthur D. Little's Michael figures equipment alone could be worth $50 billion to $70 billion, with as much as half of that going to the Japanese.

Isn't software a Japanese weakness? Yes, but not forever. "The Japanese know software is their weakness, so they're drawing on the West and Eastern Europe [Hungary]," says M. Eugene Merchant, a respected authority on factory automation.

"The big show will be the new $800 million Toyota plant [due for completion in Kentucky in mid-1988]," says Franco Eleuteri, director of advanced facility projects for the Austin Co. "If the rumors I've heard are true, it will be revolutionary." Breath is being held: Toyota has not yet awarded the construction contract, but Ohbayashi is said to be the front-runner.

WHERE THE JOBS ARE[3]

Forget, for the moment, the droning debate about trade. Forget posturing politicians, bewildering economists, exchange rates, howls about protectionism, hollow pledges of international economic cooperation. Instead, consider that this week is Dianna Ginn's last at Hermies, a popular diner in Marysville, Ohio, a small company town in the cradle of America's rust belt. For four

[3]Reprint of an article by Bill Powell, *Newsweek* staffwriter. Reprinted by permission from *Newsweek*, v. 109:42–8. February 2, 1987. Copyright © 1987 by Newsweek, Inc.

years the 41-year-old divorced mother of three has earned $2.40 an hour plus tips waiting on workers from the local factory—wishing all the while she had one of their high-paying jobs. On Jan. 21, three years after submitting her application, Ginn got the job she wanted. On Feb. 2 she starts working on the assembly line at the Honda Motor Corp. of America. "You talk about the American dream," said one of Ginn's customers at Hermies, "well, this is the Marysville dream: working for Honda."

Working for Honda. Or, in Norman, Okla., for Hitachi, or in La Vergne, Tenn., for Bridgestone Tire or in Perryville, Mo., for Toyoda Gosei. In communities across the United States, Japan Inc. holds out the "Help Wanted" sign and eager American workers sign on in droves. In 1986 the estimated U.S. trade deficit with Japan soared to $60 billion, but Japan's direct investment in the United States also shot up. The Japanese poured around $27 billion into plant, equipment and real estate—investment that created tens of thousands of American jobs. According to the best statistics available, nearly 250,000 Americans work for Japan Inc., making it one of the largest and the fastest-growing employers in the United States. Tokyo's Ministry of International Trade and Industry predicts Japanese investment will spawn an additional 840,000 American jobs in the next decade—an estimate some analysts consider conservative.

The surging Japanese investment comes at a delicate moment in U.S.-Japanese relations. Washington's irritation with Japan's economic policy has seldom been greater, and vice versa. Last week Japan's finance minister, Kiichi Miyazawa, hurried to Washington for an emergency meeting with U.S. Treasury Secretary James A. Baker III. Miyazawa came to discuss the U.S. dollar's continuing collapse against the yen. Why was he so worried? A rising yen hurts in two ways. By making Japanese products more expensive, it could cripple the country's export-led economy. A strong yen also makes it more attractive for Japanese companies to invest here than at home. But the Baker-Miyazawa discussions resulted in no new agreements, and the dollar continued to weaken against the yen.

For the United States, that is not necessarily bad news. It means the torrent of Japanese investment won't ebb anytime soon. Japan's money represents a huge vote of confidence in the U.S. economy. And with the money comes new plants, more jobs, new technologies and, perhaps most important, a management philosophy that's arguably more equitable and efficient than any other. The amount of Japanese investment here will inevitably stir controversy. "But the issue shouldn't even be debated," says the Brookings Institution's Edward Lincoln. "Their trade surplus is going to be reduced more by direct investment [abroad] than it is by change in their domestic market anyway."

The Japanese will no longer be the inscrutable, seemingly invulnerable economic rival across the ocean. They will be across the street, producing in the United States, employing American workers and managers in ever-greater numbers, operating under U.S. laws and regulations—just like American companies. A decade from now, in fact, today's debate about the U.S.-Japanese trade problem may seem strangely anachronistic. Many American workers won't be concerned with slapping tariffs of Japanese goods or with what an "appropriate" yen-dollar exchange rate is. Instead, they'll wonder if they should work for Japan Inc.—or invite their Japanese boss over for dinner.

In the eyes of many Americans, the billions of yen pouring into the United States only adds to Japan's image as an indomitable economic machine. The image and the reality, however, are now very different. The soaring yen is a boot on the neck of an economy dependent on exports, but it is hardly the only problem the Japanese confront. In fact, they face ailments that have afflicted the United States since the late 1970s: slowing domestic demand for a wide range of capital goods and stiff competition from countries with significantly lower labor costs. Throw in the threat of new protectionist barriers in the United States, says Kazuo Nukazawa of the Japan Federation of Economic Organizations, and many Japanese companies face a stark choice: "Invest overseas or perish."

No Sympathy

Don't feel too sorry for Japan, though. The nation simply has more money than it knows what to do with. The Japanese save money at an astonishing rate; of the 10 largest banks in the world, seven are in Japan. Moreover, many of the country's biggest industrial companies have so much cash "that they look like banks," as one U.S. investment banker says. The upshot: Japan may create jobs at a rapid clip in the United States for years to come. "Direct investment will be a tidal wave, but it's only starting now," says Eugene Atkinson, a managing director in Goldman Sachs & Co.'s Tokyo office.

The effects of that investment will be profound—for both the United States and Japan. Today Japan's most visible U.S. presence is in autos and consumer electronics. Conceivably, Japanese firms one day may be employers of choice in Silicon Valley and perhaps even on Wall Street, the citadel of American capitalism. And each time a major Japanese company locates a plant or an office in the United States, its major suppliers are not far behind. As a consequence, U.S. companies will face more intense competition in their own backyard. For many American businessmen, it's time to put up or shut up. Some U.S. manufacturers have pinned their economic woes on their rivals across the Pacific. U.S. companies have often accused the Japanese of pricing below cost and dumping their products into the U.S. market illegally. Now some American companies will have more than the "level playing field" they have so desired. They'll have the home-court advantage. Japan's investment in the United States "is a challenge to us," says Lincoln. "If we can't meet it, well, we deserve to work for the Japanese."

The Japanese, too, will be severely tested. They must prove they can put an American face on their vaunted consensus-management style. They will have to manage workers who believe corporate loyalty means showing up for work on time—not spending a lifetime married to a company. "Most Americans are very, very individualistic—you could almost say egotistic; they are quite different from the way we would like our people to be," concedes Asa Jonishi, senior director of Kyocera Corp., a Japanese high-tech company with U.S. operations in southern California. The president of the Building and Construction Trades Department of the AFL-CIO mocks the paternalistic style of Japanese companies: "We're the father and you're the children," says Robert Georgine. "'We'll tell you what's good for you, and you do everything you can to make us successful.' That doesn't wash here," he asserts.

Vast Differences

Few people are so willing to dismiss the Japanese system. It may be the most productive management style in history, and an increasing number of workers and managers believe the we're-all-in-this-together attitude works just as well in the United States. Still, the cultural differences *are* vast. In some U.S. industries independent trade unions are a fact of life. So too—in every industry—are smart, assertive women. The Japanese have little experience at home with either, and that's painfully obvious to U.S. employees of Japan's biggest companies. Two weeks ago Sumitomo Corp. of America settled a sex-discrimination suit filed by a dozen former women workers. The suit alleged Sumitomo restricted women to clerical positions, never promoting them to sales and management jobs. Under the settlement—which was widely viewed as almost unconditional surrender for Sumitomo—the company promised to increase sharply the number of women in sales and management. The AFL-CIO also won a dispute recently with a major Japanese company. Toyota and its prime contractor agreed to allow union workers to build a new auto plant now under construction in Georgetown, Ky. The union had staged a public campaign of harassment to force Toyota's Japanese contractor to hire union workers.

Bitter, publicized disputes horrify the Japanese, and they go to great lengths to avoid them. The settlement with the AFL-CIO will cost Toyota millions in additional construction costs, but the company settled to get the publicity behind it. As the Japanese presence in the United States increases, more public battles are inevitable. Even in Marysville there are people who object to Honda's presence. Some don't like what the Japanese did to Pearl Harbor; others, what they did to Detroit.

The most important task Japanese managers face is to defuse the tension. Their first step is often to minimize the Japanese presence in the company. Yuzaburo Mogi, managing director of Kikkoman Corp., a Japanese food company with a subsidiary in Wisconsin, recently wrote that "no matter how eager Americans may seem in getting Japanese investment, the failure to go local [hire Americans] may provoke a backlash and turn the welcoming mood to an anti-Japanese specter." Mogi insists that his Japanese employees working in the United States mix with local people; they must also live dispersed throughout the community and not in "Little Tokyo" ghettos.

The Japanese presence, measured by numbers, is minimal at most American subsidiaries. At Nissan Motor's Smyrna, Tenn., plant there are only 13 Japanese executives at a facility that employs 3,300. At Matsushita's huge electronics plant in Chicago, there are only a handful of Japanese executives and engineers. Numbers, however, do not equate to influence and power. Indeed, "numbers are largely irrelevant," says Thomas McCraw, a professor at the Harvard Business School and editor of a new book on the U.S.-Japan economic rivalry. McCraw believes Japan's success here will hinge on how successfully its companies delegate real responsibility to American managers and workers. Failure to do so, he argues, will cause debilitating morale problems.

Nomura Securities International, the largest Japanese stock-brokerage firm, found that out the hard way. Current and former employees say a bitter dispute at the firm a year ago resulted, in part, from simmering tension between Japanese managers and some American traders. Every Monday in Nomura's New York office senior traders met with top managers, ostensibly to discuss important management issues. "Instead," says one former Nomura trader, "the guy running the meeting would stand up and say so-and-so has a birthday this week and so-and-so is going out to Los Angeles to meet with someone from another firm—totally irrelevant stuff." Then, former employees say, after that meeting broke up each week, the top Japanese officials trooped off into another room and held *another* meeting. "It was consensus management all right," adds a current Nomura insider, "a consensus of the Japanese." Nomura brought in new management after several traders left the firm, and insiders say the atmosphere, though still less than ideal, has improved significantly.

Wielding Power

What happened at Nomura is relatively rare. But the perception that Americans can never attain positions of power hurts Japanese companies trying to do business here. It prevents them from hiring top-level management talent in the United States. A more realistic concern for title-conscious American executives is that upward mobility in a Japanese firm will be limited. The president in most cases is going to be Japanese. Still, Americans can wield power. Consensus management often strips much of the meaning from titles. Says Pat Park, assistant general manager of Haseko, the Los Angeles subsidiary of a Japanese real-estate development company: "There are many times when I'm the janitor here, picking up rubbish. But there are also many times when major decisions are made because I say so. There's more equity in Japanese companies."

Americans hold key positions at several of the biggest Japanese companies in the world. At Daiwa Securities in New York, vice chairman Paul Aron's authority is undisputed. He is a respected Wall Street veteran, and Daiwa's Tokyo office seeks his opinion on a wide range of management issues. At Nissan Motors in Smyrna, Americans are also in control. President Marvin Runyon and director of product quality Joe Desarla spent 37 and 14 years, respectively, at Ford. "We're not a Japanese company," insists Runyon; "we're an American company." Desarla says Nissan in America retains what Detroit did well, dumps what it did poorly and adopts some of the Japanese philosophy on the shop floor. The plant, operating since 1983, is nearly as productive as its sister plants in Japan.

In manufacturing industries, the shop floor is where the competitive battles are won or lost. In the United States, they have mostly been lost. But as one American executive working for a Japanese company in Tokyo says, "Where the Japanese go for hearts and minds is not in the boardroom, but on the shop floor." Their ability to manage a manufacturing operation transcends national borders. At New United Motors in Fremont, Calif., Toyota and GM together successfully revamped an auto plant in the shell of a strife-torn GM factory closed in 1982. And unlike Nissan in Smyrna, Fremont is a union shop—though one with remarkably few work rules and hierarchy.

Not every Japanese company that builds or buys a plant here will operate flawlessly. The United States is still a tough environment in which to manufacture efficiently. For that reason, argues Tokyo-based McKinsey & Co. consultant Kenichi Ohmae, some Japanese companies will fail.

Bottom Lines

The best companies—the Sonys and the Toyotas—won't. They can make quality goods at competitive prices anywhere. More Japan-in-America success stories are inevitable. For Americans the question is, whose success is it: theirs, or ours? The correct answer—in a world in which capital crosses borders at the touch of a computer key—is that the *question* is becoming irrelevant. Nissan worker J. R. McGowan understands that better than most. "When I was hired," he says, "I wore my Nissan uniform everywhere, and some people stopped me and asked if I was working for those 'blank, blank' Japanese." In time, though, the hostility diminished. "The bottom line," says McGowan, "is that I'm building a truck somebody's going to be riding in. I might be driving this truck, so I'm going to do it right."

In the late 1960s the United States dominated the world economically. In a book called "The American Challenge," French journalist Jean-Jacques Servan-Schreiber foresaw dire consequences for a Europe overwhelmed by American investment and ingenuity. Sitting by helplessly, he wrote, the Europeans would see "American investment skim gently across the earth . . . and watch what it takes away." Japan today is a great economic power with a vast amount of money to invest around the globe. But Europe today is hardly an American economic colony; companies such as Ford and IBM are simply part of the economic landscape, like Renault or Siemens. Americans probably don't need to worry about what Japanese investment "will take away." It won't take away much—and people like Dianna Ginn will be too busy making money to notice anyway.

LOVE AND HATE IN AMERICA[4]

The tables have turned on foreign investment in America. For decades it was American firms that bought foreign rivals and set up factories around the world. Now it is the foreigners writing the cheques. According to the Japan External Trade Organisation, foreigners increased their holdings of American land, factories and companies by 13% in 1987, to $209 billion. They are fast closing on the $250 billion of direct investment which Americans have accumulated abroad.

The Japanese have been among the busiest shoppers. In 1987 Japan's new direct investment in America nearly doubled, to $23 billion. Although this left Japan a distant third in America's direct investment league table—behind Britain's $51 billion and

[4]Reprint of a staffwritten article. Copyright © 1988 The Economist Newspaper Ltd. All rights reserved.

Holland's $43 billion—it has landed them in the middle of the foreign-investment controversy.

Last year the Reagan administration blocked Fujitsu's proposed takeover of Fairchild, an American chipmaker and subsidiary of France's Schlumberger. In this election year emotional appeals to regulate foreign investment—for vague reasons like "preserving America's economic independence"—have won some surprising backers, among them a New York investment banker, Mr. Felix Rohatyn. But foreign investment has some equally surprising advocates. Democratic presidential candidate Mr. Dick Gephardt defends East Asian investment in America as staunchly as he denounces East Asian imports.

A poor showing by Mr. Gephardt on Super Tuesday has removed some of the pressure on Congress to pass protectionist trade legislation. But politicians are still hotly debating proposals to regulate foreign investment, or at least to register it. A recent poll by Smick-Medley & Associates, a consultancy firm based in Washington, D.C., found that 40% of American citizens favoured a ban on foreign investment.

In the absence of federal regulation, it is up to individual states to decide who they want to encourage to set up shop within their borders. Whatever the doubts in Congress, most states are busily encouraging job-creating foreigners—in particular the Japanese. The Smick-Medley poll indicates that the Japanese are far and away Americans' favourite foreign employers.

Forty states have offices in Tokyo to woo investors. The sales pitch can include a variety of incentives: near all states offer to cut red tape for Japanese investors; some offer to build roads and other infrastructure, although that depends on the project; some provide financial incentives like tax privileges or industrial development bonds at low interest rates. Oregon supports a Japanese school in Portland.

The result has been a smorgasbord of opportunity for Japanese investors. They have concentrated on regional specialities. In Hawaii they have bought up about half of the resort hotels. In Oregon they are setting up electronics plants. In Ohio, Illinois and Indiana they have bought or set up engineers and metal-bashers. In New York the money has gone into financial firms, and everywhere the Japanese have quietly been buying or setting up the wholesale distribution networks for their imports. But the most sought after prizes have been the biggest employers: car-makers.

For large, high-visibility projects like these, competition between states can create big incentives. Toyota's plant in Kentucky was greeted with $112m-worth of new roads, low-cost loans, employee training and 1,500 acres of free land. Foreign takeover artists cannot count on such a warm welcome. Ohio fought tooth and nail against the attempted takeover of Goodyear by Sir James Goldsmith, an Anglo-French financier—even as the state's governor Mr. Dick Celeste worked to complete a deal for Ohio's second Honda plant. While Sir James threatened to reduce jobs by restructuring Goodyear, the Japanese are steady job creators.

According to JETRO, Japanese firms and their affiliates provide 160,000 jobs in America. Their style of investment reassures local American bureaucrats. By and large the Japanese avoid hostile takeovers, with an occasional exception like Dainippon Ink's $540m contested takeover of Reichold Chemical. They are willing to take long-term minority stakes rather than seek full control. Indeed such minority investments are Japan's favourite sort of deal with financial firms.

In manufacturing, the typical Japanese investment will be a green-field start-up, which then grows fast. That is less contentious than buying an existing American firm. For the past three years, Japan has been America's biggest foreign investor in terms of the number of companies investing (though third by value of investments). Mr. David McKay, Ohio's development director, reports that the majority of Japanese investments in his state begin life with perhaps three or four Japanese employees and 40–50 Americans, and they look at least to double employment in five years. Oregon expects its 350 Japanese firms almost to triple their initial investments of $300m, and to expand employment from 25,000 today to 65,000 by 1993.

There are still some problems between Japanese firms and the natives. Despite much publicised successes for Japanese management techniques—like the Californian GM plant rescued by Toyota—the differences between the American and Japanese way of doing business require some effort to overcome.

Ask a Japanese businessman what is his greatest problem in working in America and he is likely to cite the difficulty of getting good components. Conspiracy theorists say this is an excuse to bring in Japanese component suppliers, but there is a genuinely sharp contrast between Japan's tradition of long-term relationships with suppliers and America's more free-wheeling ways. Japanese techniques of just-in-time inventory management often require suppliers to invest in new equipment to win a contract. So do their product designs. American suppliers are reluctant to invest.

For those Americans who do learn to deal with their new neighbours, the rewards can be great. In effect, they are learning how to compete internationally while still at home. Some think they can seize new opportunities to export to Japan, helped by experience with their new Japanese customers in America.

II. AMERICAN COMPANIES IN JAPAN

EDITOR'S INTRODUCTION

In turning from Japan's easy access to the American domestic market to American companies doing business in Japan, a rather different situation presents itself. By long established tradition, Japan has discouraged foreign penetration of its home markets through a complicated system of government regulations, tariffs, and other import barriers. An element of xenophobia may well be involved in this system of protectionism, but it is also part of the Japanese psychology of business, in which quality control is built in through long, close business relationships—an arrangement of consensus that can be relied upon and trusted. The Japanese home market is not impenetrable by foreign business interests, but they have had to learn how to adapt to a Japanese style of doing business. Those that have learned this lesson have been able to achieve gradual but steady success.

In the first article in this section, Kathleen K. Wiegner in *Forbes* explains how IBM has scored notable success in the Japanese home market. Indeed, its wholly owned Japanese subsidiary, IBM Japan Ltd., has surged ahead to the point where it almost shares the domestic market evenly with its great Japanese rival Fujitsu. The key to IBM's success, as Wiegner points out, is that the company has learned to tailor its computers and computer software to Japanese needs, developing a technology, for example, that accommodates the transmission of *kanji*, or Japan's thousands of characters. Barbara Rudolph's article in *Time* reports on other American companies that have managed to flourish in Japan despite government and business restrictions. They have done so, again, by catering to Japanese preferences and tastes, by patience and determination. A concluding article by Joel Dreyfuss in *Fortune* notes that a number of Japanese markets are still closed to foreigners. The Japanese are still strongly protective of their agriculture and construction industries, and American companies have still made no inroads into such other industries as supercomputers and medical equipment. Yet in other fields American companies, ranging from Kodak film to Kellogg cereals, have managed to establish presences in the domestic market. The strong yen has given U.S. business the best price-cutting edge it has had in decades.

"A FINE JAPANESE COMPANY"[1]

Others wring their hands over the U.S.' $37 billion (and growing) trade deficit with Japan. A few U.S. companies are doing something about it. IBM, for example. Its wholly owned Japanese subsidiary, IBM Japan Ltd., sold an estimated $3 billion worth of computer gear last year, a 25% increase over 1983, more than double the 1980 level. IBM Japan? Didn't *Business Week*, a well-known U.S. publication, recently report, in sadness, that the subsidiary had fallen to second place, behind Fujitsu, in the Japanese market? That story was a few years behind the facts. Fujitsu overtook IBM Japan back in 1979, but right now the race is a draw. IBM Japan trails Fujitsu by a mere $28 million in a market where each will probably do $4 billion this year. IBM is still maintaining a good lead over two formidable competitors, NEC and Hitachi.

A key to IBM's success in this tough market is its willingness to tailor products especially to Japanese requirements. "In 1973," recalls Takeo Shiina, the affable president of IBM Japan, in his fluent English, "Frank Cary [IBM chairman at the time] asked me what was happening in Japan. I started my presentation with two photographs, one of a street corner in the Ginza right after the war, and the second of the same corner in 1973. In the first picture all you see are U.S. Army jeeps and trucks. In the latter picture just Japanese cars. I told him how the Japanese auto industry developed. 'Please, pay attention,' I said, 'because pretty soon computers will be the same.'"

Under Shiina's prodding and Fujitsu's challenge, IBM did pay attention. Says Stephen Cohen, a vice president at the Gartner Group, a research firm: "IBM finally realized the Japanese market is unique."

[1]Reprint of an article by Kathleen K. Wiegner, *Forbes* staffwriter. Reprinted by permission of *Forbes* magazine, April 8, 1985. Copyright © Forbes, Inc., 1985.

The result has been a steady stream of products designed specifically for Japanese users, often by Japanese engineers. To combat a surging NEC, IBM Japan first introduced the 5550 workstation in 1983, then the JX personal computer in 1984, both capable of handling Japan's thousands of characters, or *kanji*. While *kanji*-handling printers and displays had been developed in the U.S., the 5550 was designed almost exclusively in Japan, at IBM Japan's Fujisawa Development Laboratories.

The 5550 has taken off in Japan as IBM's PC has in the U.S. In 1983 the 5550 won MITI's Good Product Design award, the first IBM product ever to win such an award. No one is resting on his laurels. IBM Japan just introduced the 5540, a cheaper version of 5550, and a more powerful small business computer is in the works.

The people who run IBM in Armonk, N.Y. were wise enough to listen to what their people on the spot were saying. Hence IBM's decision to conduct basic research in Japan. "When I talked about it, they said, 'Why do you need research? Why not send it to Yorktown?'" say Nobuo Mii, managing director for technical operations, recalling his suggestion that IBM add Tokyo to San Jose, Yorktown Heights, N.Y. and Zurich as centers for basic research. "So I showed them what Yorktown was doing and what our Japanese competitors were doing. The Japanese [competitors] were working on character recognition, image processing, language translation. I said, 'This kind [of research] is fundamental to staying in Japan.'"

Armonk, in 1982, established IBM Japan's Japan Science Institute, tucked away beyond the far side of the Imperial Palace in Tokyo. This is commercial science on a high level. Today 155 people working under Research Director Hisashi Kobayashi are attempting to develop a better version of *kanji* software; image processing technology, so that written text can be entered into a computer through a scanning device rather than with a keyboard; and artificial intelligence.

When it came to producing the model 5550, Mii again displayed some of IBM Japan's strategic thinking by turning to giant Matsushita Electric for the actual manufacturing. "Matsushita historically had worked with IBM on display terminals," explains Mii. "They have OEM experience and good knowhow on how to reduce costs." For keyboards IBM Japan went to Alps Electric; for components to companies like Hitachi; for printers to Oki Electric. The 5550, in other words, is a truly Japanese product under an American nameplate.

IBM Japan has its own factories, of course. These are in Yasu, near Lake Biwa, and Fujisawa, an hour's train ride from Tokyo. A visitor to Fujisawa, for example, cannot but notice the clean room where white-masked women assemble disk drives for IBM's XT computer.

How did these drives come to be made at Fujisawa? Here's how Kerisaku Nomura, Fujisawa's plant manager, tells the story:

"About two years ago IBM's San Jose operation was looking for a manufacturer for the XT drive and thought a Japanese company might be a good source. So we raised our hands and said, 'Let us make it. We are a Japanese company, too.' So we made a study of technical feasibility and cost and came up with a plan that showed we were competitive." Nomura's plant began producing XT drives in June, the only IBM plant in the world making drives for the XT. Current production is all shipped to the U.S.

Shina has convinced IBM to price aggressively. IBM used to convert a product's dollar price into yen and tacked on a bit to reflect the cost of doing business internationally. During the 1970s this policy produced good profits but left IBM vulnerable to undercutting by competitors. Now IBM has cut prices. Shiina, in other words, has persuaded his bosses in Armonk to sacrifice short-term profit for the long-term market share. How Japanese can you get?

As smaller, less-expensive computer systems became a larger part of IBM Japan's business, new channels of distribution had to be found. In 1982 IBM Japan began setting up a network of independent Japanese dealers—*dairiten*, as they're called—who buy IBM computers and resell them to customers with the appropriate software. Nippon Office Systems, a joint venture with trading company Kanematsu-Gosho, sells and services office systems.

In computers, as elsewhere, the Japanese government is brilliant at throwing up hard-to-detect trade barriers for the benefit of Japanese manufacturers. One such is JECC, a third-party leasing company, backed by the Japanese government, exclusively for Japanese computer makers. To combat this advantage, IBM made a deal with Morgan Guaranty International Finance and Orient Leasing Co. (Japan's largest leasing company) that provides IBM Japan with much of the same facilities JECC offers the purely Japanese companies.

Last year IBM reorganized its Americas/Far East subsidiary, forming a new central organization called Asia/Pacific Group, headquartered less than a mile from IBM Japan's own headquarters. George Conrades, a 23-year IBM veteran with a strong marketing background, moved in to head up APG. With him came around 200 non-Japanese IBMers.

The Japanese press has had a field day feeding rumors to the always xenophobic Japanese. Cartoons of Conrades dressed like General Douglas MacArthur, down to the corncob pipe, circulate along with stories that Shiina's job is on the line.

One wonders whether this kind of paranoia isn't encouraged by IBM's Japanese competitors. The competitors are frankly worried. IBM Japan is ready to make its big push to win back market share. Conrades is not in Tokyo to second-guess his Japanese counterparts but rather to help build sales. "There is no way we can establish the customer relationship that a Japanese sales guy can," says Conrades. What he can do, he says, is "support" IBM Japan's marketing effort—meaning turn up the heat somewhat on the subsidiary's salesmen and narrow the communication gap between Armonk and Tokyo. In short, Conrades is there to support IBM Japan, not to run it.

While APG is headquartered in Tokyo, its responsibility extends to all of Southeast Asia, Australia and New Zealand. IBM has big plans for this market, particularly now that is has products specific to the Asia business. The 5550 has been outfitted with software that handles *hanzi*, the Chinese characters, and which is being offered to Taiwan, Hong Kong, even mainland China.

Takeo Shiina's eyes twinkle when he recalls what happened when he distributed translated copies of Thomas Watson Jr.'s book *A Business and Its Beliefs* to his Japanese business associates: "The president of Nissan Motors said to me after he had read the book, 'Shiina-san, here is a fine Japanese company, operating outside of Japan.'"

WINNERS AGAINST TOUGH ODDS[2]

For decades American firms have complained that a formidable array of government regulations, tariffs and other import barriers in Japan are as difficult to fathom as a formal tea ceremony, effectively blocking business there. Nonetheless, many U.S. companies have flourished in that environment, playing by the rules and somehow still coming out ahead. IBM Japan's 1985 sales might reach $2.7 billion, up about 20% from last year. Schick claims 70% of the safety-razor market. This year U.S. firms will export $25 billion worth of products to Japan. Proclaims Herbert Hayde, president of the American Chamber of Commerce in Tokyo: "American manufacturers are alive and well in Japan."

U.S. companies that do business successfully in Japan, including such household names as Coca-Cola and Elizabeth Arden, began with a firm commitment to crack the market, however long it might take. "If the Japanese get the impression that you're not committed to business for the long term, you're in trouble," says Robert J. Sievers, who just completed a three-year stint as president of Du Pont Japan. Echoes James Abegglen, director of the Graduate School of Comparative Culture at Tokyo's Sophia University: "There must be a conviction that says you are going to be in Japan, by God, whatever it takes."

Foreign businessmen learn that in Japan profitmaking requires patience. In the U.S., deals may be struck over a single lunch, but Japanese executives feel comfortable only after extended contact. Says Albert Sieg, president of Kodak Japan: "The worst mistake is to tell your prospective business partners that your plane leaves at 2 p.m. Friday, and you have to clinch a deal by then."

Finding and keeping a good distributor can be crucial. Consider how Schick captured its sizable share of Japan's $200 million safety-razor market. In the early 1960s, Schick and its rival Gillette began selling their razor blades in Japan. Both faced keen competition from Feather, a Japanese manufacturer. Schick de-

---

[2]Reprint of an article by Barbara Rudolph, *Time* staffwriter. Reprinted by permission from *Time*, December 9, 1985. Copyright © 1985 Time Inc.

cided to retain a prominent local distributor, Hattori. But Gillette blundered by abandoning its local agent after a few years. Japanese retailers viewed Gillette's move as arrogant, and the firm was unable to sell its products on its own. Says Jay Gwynne, president of the consumer health-products division of Warner-Lambert, which owns Schick: "To try to eliminate the Japanese middleman is the quickest way to commit suicide." Schick's single-blade stainless-steel razor was judged superior to Feather's double-blade carbon one, and Schick's razor became the country's best seller.

Some successes are built on old-fashioned ingenuity. One recent example is Ore-Ida Foods, which makes frozen potatoes, little known in Japan until the firm arrived a year ago. Ore-Ida, a division of H. J. Heinz, had conducted surveys that revealed that busy Japanese working women had a hunger for easily prepared frozen foods. The company also showed a willingness to change its ingredients in order to please its new customers. The frozen fries in Tokyo are made with less salt than those sold in the U.S. Reason: the Japanese prefer to sprinkle the seasoning themselves. After only one year of business, Ore-Ida now claims 11% of the $40 million market.

That kind of attention to detail helped auto-parts maker Borg-Warner, which discovered that the Japanese believe a product must look good even if the customer will never see it. Borg-Warner, a manufacturing conglomerate, makes a five-speed transmission used in Nissan's popular 280Z and 300ZX sports cars. While the driver sees only the stick shift, Nissan insisted that the whole transmission must shine. "We ran into the Japanese fetish for appearance," says Thomas Hague, the firm's Asian area director. "It's an emotional thing with them." After Borg-Warner polished up its act, Nissan was happy.

IBM remains the largest and most successful American company in Japan. It controls an estimated 26% of the computer market, which makes it a close second to Fujitsu, whose shares is 28%. The reason is IBM's consistent ability to create computers that appeal to the specific needs of the Japanese consumer.

Success, however, has not come without a struggle. Last month IBM said that it has submitted to arbitration a claim against Fujitsu for copying and selling software that is similar to IBM's products. The American manufacturer maintains that Fujitsu is violating a 1983 agreement between the two firms. IBM also went through a corporate reorganization in which 200 U.S. employees were transferred to IBM's Asia/Pacific Group as part of an effort to boost sales.

IBM, AT&T and other high-tech firms are now vying with one another to tap into Japan's telecommunications market. Last April, Japan's national telephone system was converted from a state-run monopoly into a private enterprise. While it is too soon to predict how much business will be captured by foreign firms, the winners are likely to be those companies that can adapt to the special demands of the Japanese market. Says Byron Battle, an undersecretary of economic affairs for the Massachusetts Office of International Trade: "In Japan, you have to sell it their way, not the Great American way." That is a lesson as old as world trade.

HOW TO BEAT THE JAPANESE AT HOME[3]

Has there ever been a more inviting time for Americans to try selling in Japan? The powerful yen gives them the best price-cutting opportunity in decades, and the Japanese government is grudgingly opening long-closed markets. At last Yanks have a fighting chance to sway the intensely loyal customers in a vast economy second only to the U.S.

There's just one problem: Japan may be the toughest sell on earth. For Westerners the language is notoriously difficult, customs and manners baffling, attitudes frostily insular. As some markets open, many others remain locked. U.S. trade negotiators say that for now foreigners can pretty much forget about competing in agriculture, construction, and sales to the government; to that list, a U.S. electronics industry association adds the manufacturing of supercomputers, medical equipment, high-purity silicon, and wireless communications equipment. Yet several U.S. companies have overcome the seemingly insurmountable difficulties, and a fast-growing number of newcomers are trying. The

[3]Reprint of an article by Joel Dreyfuss, *Fortune* staffwriter. Reprinted by permission from *Fortune*, August 31, 1987. Copyright © 1987 Time Inc. All rights reserved.

American Chamber of Commerce in Japan has over 1,600 members—500 of them new since 1982.

With the Japanese market more alluring than ever, U.S. companies are finding new ways to apply simple rules Japan experts have been preaching for a generation: Foreign companies must have a commitment to quality, a willingness to adjust to the market, a long view, and strong support from the home office. Just as important, they must avoid certain businesses and win the Japanese government to their side.

The hardest part of entering many Japanese industries is breaking down official barriers, which often seems impossible. But take heart: It can be done, perhaps more easily now than ever. Japan lifted restrictions against foreign cigarette sales last year, and U.S. tobacco companies have since doubled their share of business in the biggest non-Communist market where the antismoking movement is still weak. Says Guy Aelvoet, the chain-smoking Belgian president of Philip Morris in Japan: "We're playing on a level field now."

Smoothing the field took a decade of steady political spadework, culminating in a threat of sanctions by the Reagan Administration. Japan capitulated, and foreign manufacturers are now allowed to increase imports and, for the first time, set their own retail prices. They have also been allowed to advertise on television, which Philip Morris and others are doing aggressively. Result: Retail sales of imports climbed 50% last year, to $1.1 billion.

The yen's most recent surge enabled foreign cigarette makers to drop their prices to within a few cents of premium Japanese brands, sending sales even higher. Philip Morris's Japanese sales hit $170 million last year; in the past 12 months they rose 95%. With domestic brands holding 95% of the market and two out of three Japanese men smoking, the outlook for foreign companies is cloudless.

Inspiring Equitable Life Assurance was the knowledge that capturing just 1% of the Japanese market would create a business equal to the 15th-largest American life insurer. The company finally won Japanese government approval to launch a retail insurance business last year, but that was only a first step. Next, subsidiary president Donald Mooney worried about staffing. Few first-rate Japanese college graduates want to give up the security of lifetime employment to join foreign companies with little status and a seemingly shaky future. "The most serious concern we has was hiring Japanese professionals," he says. "All the books said we couldn't do it. But things have changed."

In a little over 18 months Mooney assembled a staff of 350 to tackle Japan's leading insurers on their home turf. He chose some of his top executives from managers traditionally forced to retire from Japanese corporations between the ages of 50 and 57; younger employees came from those who consider the possibilities for promotion in a foreign enterprise better than in a large Japanese firm. "We're very happy with the quality of people," says Mooney. His new salespeople bring in slightly bigger premiums than their novice U.S. counterparts.

Like other American executives in Japan, Mooney emphasizes the importance of convincing employees as well as potential customers that the company is committed to providing quality and service over the long haul. For that reason, his Japanese sales force ventures forth with brochures emphasizing that Equitable has been serving customers since the 19th century.

Officials at Allied Automotive, part of Allied-Signal, had heard all about Japan's maniacal pursuit of quality when they decided to go after business there in 1979. A team of executives from the group that makes brake pads, then a unit of Bendix and later taken over by Allied, flew to Japan and made the rounds of automakers. "We found them willing to talk to us but a little cool," says Patrick Thesier, group director for business development. Only two companies agreed to take product samples for engineering tests, but they were industry giants Nissan and Toyota. Nissan quickly found fault with the samples and ended discussions. But after comprehensive tests, Toyota came through with what Allied considered a very small order: 20,000 brake pads a month.

"Most U.S. companies wouldn't go through the agony of starting to do business with a Japanese company on such a small order," says Thesier, but senior management was determined to succeed in Japan. The "agony" began with the most stringent requirements Allied executives had ever seen. In addition to performance, Toyota specified the appearance of the pads: Though they were hidden from sight, they had to be painted. "We had to install painting equipment—just for Toyota," says Thesier.

Allied knew it was dealing with a different kind of customer, but it was not ready for the reaction to the first shipment. "They said, 'You didn't comply. We are sending the parts back,'" recalls Thesier, who says some dimensions were off by a few thousandths of an inch. If U.S. companies had noticed such small discrepancies they would still have accepted the parts, since the flaws did not affect performance. Toyota's reaction sent a shock through Thesier's division. "When you fail with a U.S. customer," he says, "you can count on a dispensation to fix the problem." Toyota's only concession was to tell Allied that it would accept those parts that met its exact specifications. The U.S. company flew the manager of its brake pad plant to Japan to sort good parts from bad, a gesture that, Thesier observes in retrospect, "sent a message about our commitment."

Allied took a year adjusting to Toyota's quality requirements, says Thesier, and the effort paid off. Toyota now buys 200,000 brake pads a month—about 20% of its total—from Allied. When the Japanese carmaker started the New United Motor Manufacturing joint venture with GM in California in 1983, Allied supplied pads. The company hopes to sell them to Toyota when it begins making cars in Kentucky next year. Allied's status as a Toyota supplier has opened doors: Honda and Nissan are testing Allied pads, and Thesier is talking to Fuji Heavy Industries, maker of Subaru.

Apple Computer started selling personal computers in Japan almost as soon as they sprang from the minds of Steven Jobs and Stephen Wozniak in the late 1970s. But it did not sell many. Most instruction manuals were in English, and the software would not work with the complex set of Chinese characters and phonetic symbols used in written Japanese. Apple had no organized marketing effort and left sales completely in the hands of local distributors. In 1983 Apple established a Japanese subsidiary to back its sales efforts, but it named three presidents in three years, the worst way to instill confidence in Japanese customers, who are used to orderly corporate successions. Concedes Alexander van Eyck, president of Apple Japan since 1986: "We were not enjoying the kind of success in Japan that we could have."

Apple's turnaround began last year when the company finally unveiled KanjiTalk (Kanji refers to Chinese characters), a Japanese-language operating system for the company's Macintosh computer, and announced that several key software developers, including Microsoft, had agreed to convert their software to the new system. Van Eyck says the introduction dramatically changed attitudes about Apple and hugely expanded its market. Then the company took advantage of the strong yen and cut the price of the U.S.-made Macintosh Plus from $4,600 to under $3,000. Sales are 100% head of last year's, according to van Eyck—an industry analyst puts them at $1 million to $1.5 million—and profits up 600%. After trailing Australia and New Zealand for years, "Japan is fast becoming our largest Pacific market," says van Eyck. "We're gearing up for a tremendous leap forward."

Kodak is fighting to regain lost glory. In the 1920s Kodak was the best-known name in film and cameras in Japan. But World War II cut off business, and Kodak did not reestablish its Japanese subsidiary until 1963. Its marketing efforts remained low-key and half-hearted.

In the past three years Kodak has pushed aggressively to recover the color film business it surrendered to Japanese archrival Fuji Photo Film. A flurry of joint ventures, aggressive marketing, and heavy promotion have made Kodak part of the Japanese vocabulary once more. In step with its parent's strategy, Kodak Japan has been investing in a variety of high-tech ventures, including a floppy-disk manufacturing operation with Mitsubishi Kasei and R&D projects in electronic imaging technology.

In the film fight the American challenger has sponsored sports events, advertised heavily, and set up kiosks at big tourist attractions (such as the Sapporo Snow Festival) to reestablish Kodak in Japanese minds. The biggest weapon in the battle is the Kodak blimp, which cruises the skies of Japan and has vied with a rival Fuji blimp for the hearts and yen of Japanese consumers. Industry analysts say that while Kodak holds over 90% of the professional slide film market, it owns only 10% to 15% of the much larger consumer film business.

Ancient habit, not a powerful company, is Kellogg's main adversary. For 25 years the cereal maker has been trying to persuade the Japanese to trade their traditional breakfast of soybean soup, egg, rice, and fish for the snap, crackle, and pop of its products. Kellogg has penetrated the Japanese consciousness and breakfast menus enough to warrant local manufacturing of 13 cereals. The company hold 80% of the dry cereal market and employs 160 in its wholly owned subsidiary.

But by Kellogg's standard, Japan has not yet begun to eat. The average Japanese consumes only 1.8 ounces of breakfast cereals a year, vs. nine pounds per person in the U.S. Kellogg Japan President Nobuaki Jin explains that cereals in Japan got a bad start. Just a few months before Kellogg entered the market in the early 1960s, a Japanese confectionery company launched its own cereal brand, and confused store owners placed the new product in the candy section. Says Jin: "Twenty-five years later consumers still regard cereals as snacks."

Kellogg is trying hard. Last year it introduced its first locally developed cereal, Genmai Flakes, made from whole-grain rice. It quickly became the company's third-best-selling product (behind plain cornflakes and sugar-coated flakes). The company sponsors four nationwide TV shows to reach rural areas, augmenting an established big-city sales push. Kellogg Japan has also increased the volume of its packages an average of 13% while holding prices steady. The payoff so far is a 15% revenue rise last year and a 20% pickup in this year's first half—while industry sales remain flat. Jin's goal: a box of Kellogg's in every home and annual per capita consumption of seven ounces within seven years. "If each Japanese household ate one box a week," he says pensively, "our volume would be tremendous."

No one entering the Japanese market should expect to make money quickly. As nearly every American player learns painfully, customers are remarkably suspicious of outsiders and slow to switch brands. The strong yen and new openness of markets are not a chance for fast profits but for a potentially valuable toehold. Becoming firmly established may take years. It pays to be first. When competitors follow, just think what they will be up against.

III. COMPETITION IN THE AUTOMOBILE AND HIGH-TECH INDUSTRIES

EDITOR'S INTRODUCTION

Although the economic competition between Japan and the U.S. takes in an array of industries, attention has focused particularly upon automobiles and high technology, in both of which the Japanese have made a strong leadership challenge. A five-year restriction on Japanese auto imports provided U.S. car makers with an opportunity to improve their position, and the decreased value of the dollar as against the yen has also been helpful; but Japanese penetration of the North American auto market has been increasing nonetheless. A trend of the 1980s has been for the Japanese to build their own plants in the U.S. or to establish joint ventures with the Big Three of Detroit—G.M., Ford, and Chrysler. Although Detroit executives predicted that the Japanese would find their advantage all but eliminated on a "level playing field" in America, the Japanese have in fact adapted to local conditions with remarkable success; and American auto makers find themselves in a defensive position. Moreover, the Japanese have been formidable competitors in the field of high technology, provoking an acrimonious response from the Americans who charge that the Japanese have broken fair-trade laws by refusing to open their own markets and by dumping products (selling below cost) in the international market. In both the Reagan and Bush administrations federal legislation has been enacted that retaliates with high tariffs on Japanese goods until the Japanese give evidence of complying with fair-trade laws. Competition in high technology particularly has reached a point of high tension, straining the relations between the two allies.

In the first article in Section Three, John Merwin in *Forbes* compares two automobile plants in Ohio, the new Japanese Honda facility and the antiquated American Jeep plant. In every respect the Honda plant is shown to hold an advantage. Its assembly line is streamlined so as to require less time and fewer workers to produce the same number of cars. At Jeep, worker absenteeism is high while at Honda it is merely minimal. A move toward fuller automation at Jeep that would lower production costs has been thwarted by unions, which fear a loss of jobs; but at Honda this problem has been circumvented. Cooperation between labor and management at Honda is so cordial and closely knit that unions have been unable to gain a foothold. In a second article, James B. Treece in *Business Week* explains how the Japanese have avoided union problems by building their plants in semirural areas of the Midwest. So successful have the Japanese been in this strategy, and in their management techniques of camaraderie and team spirit, that the Nissan plant in Smyrna, Tennessee recently rejected unionization by more than a 2-to-1 vote.

Several articles that follow trace the U.S.-Japanese rivalry in high technology. Eliot Marshall in *Science* discusses the accord reached in 1986 between Japan and the U.S. in respect to the semiconductor industry and under the terms of which Japan will buy more U.S. chips and discontinue price cutting. The fragile nature of the accord, however, is revealed in a following article by George Russell in *Time*. In this piece, Russell reports on the Reagan administration's sanctions in 1987 against the Japanese for failing to live up to the agreement. Another piece by Bill Powell in *Newsweek* brings the dispute up to mid 1989, when once again the Japanese have been charged with unfair trade practices. Under the so-called Super 301 law, reprisals will be taken against Japan if the trade law violations are not redressed within 18 months. Through the late 1980s trade friction between the two allies has become a major problem, one that has no easy solution and will have to be carefully managed.

A TALE OF TWO WORLDS[1]

For one factory, these are the best of times. The plant is happy, hiring, and turning out a product of remarkable—and consistent—quality.

[1]Reprint of an article by John Merwin, *Forbes* staffwriter. Reprinted by permission of *Forbes* magazine, June 16, 1986. Copyright © Forbes Inc., 1986.

For the other factory, it is quite a different story. While the plant's product, a natural in today's segmented auto market, is selling briskly, its habits and hardware are old, morale is sagging, and management threatens to close the place beginning later this month if the union doesn't make concessions. Meanwhile, Japanese competitors are coming into the market with similar products.

These two different worlds are in fact a mere 100 miles apart. One, the 3½-year-old Honda of America plant of Marysville, Ohio, stretches across a rural landscape of grass and woodlands 30 miles north of Columbus. The other, the Jeep division of American Motors Corp., lies two hours by car farther north in Toledo, the very geographic center of the Great Lakes' industrial belt. The factory's outward appearance has not changed much since it cranked out Jeeps during World War II, and it remains an enormous, inner-city-like industrial warren of old buildings and parking lots.

Productivity is a much-discussed economic term, but it also has a powerful human dimension. Why do some factories run so smoothly, while others writhe in turmoil? Does the physical condition of the plant tell the answer, or is there something more— something about the quality of the people, their orientation toward one another, their bosses and the nature of the work itself?

To find out, *Forbes* went to both the Honda and Jeep plants, so near and yet so far away.

We began at Honda, on a Thursday afternoon, where we found Vice President Al Kinzer addressing an orientation audience of 22 new workers. "You're now in the auto business," says Kinzer. "So let me read you a few recent headlines: Ford lays off 1,450. American Motors is idle for two weeks. At Chrysler they've got 89 days' inventory. GM's got 85 and Ford has 58. At Honda, we've got 8."

Staring back at Kinzer are young faces, many of them female. Most of the new recruits wear jeans, neatly pressed cotton shirts and jogging shoes. They are starting to work next week on the factory floor at $10.60 an hour, and from the headlines Kinzer has just read aloud, they've already gotten the first of many messages Honda will deliver as time passes: $10.60 per hour is a nice enough starting pay, but job security is even nicer.

Now, for a remarkable change, drive to Jeep, first gliding across central Ohio's grassy carpet, studded with villages like

Summersville and Mount Victory. Then abruptly onto I-75, following 18-wheelers heading full throttle for Toledo and Detroit. At Jeep's 83-year-old Toledo site there are no new-employee orientations, and small wonder. Since last fall 3,000 hourly workers have been laid off, as production of one Jeep model was dropped, and the work force, built up during the launch of another model, was trimmed back.

At Jeep, productivity is hampered by old work rules, part of the baggage that comes with union contracts dating back decades. Management is pressuring the local unit of the United Auto Workers to change those rules that keep labor costs up, but the union is balking. Last year tension built to the point where a group of shop floor workers abruptly began sabotaging the assembly line, bashing Jeeps with welding tools. The line was intermittently shut down during the week that followed, costing more than $1 million in lost wages.

Honda and Jeep have one thing in common: output. Each working day Honda turns out 875 four-wheel passenger vehicles powered by internal combustion engines; Jeep produces 750 of the machines. Beyond that, the similarities end. Honda produces its vehicles in 1.7 million square feet of tightly organized floor space, while Jeep fills more than three times that amount. Honda needs 2,432 autoworkers to produce its cars. Jeep requires slightly more than twice that number.

Some of the difference is attributable to American car manufacturers' habit of offering so many options. In Toledo, Jeep makes pickups, sport vehicles and wagons. It installs two-wheel-drive, four-wheel-drive and an array of other options specified by orders attached to doors of each car coming down the line. At Marysville, Honda stamps out long runs of nearly identical cars, which is a far more efficient method.

But are there other reasons for such a wide disparity? Indeed, and one has to do with the physical layout of the plants. From where welding begins at Honda's plant until the finished car is fueled and driven off the line, no human moves the car—it is done entirely by hooks or conveyers.

At Jeep, by contrast, production lines are broken at several places, requiring carriers and partially assembled car bodies to be dragged manually from one line to the next as assembly proceeds. That not only slows production but adds employees to the payroll. The Jeep line snakes up and down through most of the factory's maze of 64 interconnected buildings, an ad hoc architectural layout that has evolved bit by bit since Willys-Overland, a name still fading from the factory's smokestacks, bought the plant in 1909.

The whole Rube Goldberg arrangement prevents Jeep from using a pure "just in time" inventory control, as Honda does. While Honda's parts inventory is largely stored by its suppliers, which deliver parts to the back dock mere hours before they are needed, Jeep requires a day or two simply to move 12,000 different parts through its labyrinth to the assembly line itself.

Much of Honda's shop floor equipment is newer and more sophisticated than Jeep's. Example: Both plants use enormous stamping machines to bend thin sheets of steel into side panels, hoods, trunk lids and other body parts. But Honda's presses, built by Danly Machine Corp., are designed so that operators can change stamping dies in less than ten minutes. At Jeep changeovers take several hours, during which employees stand around while the machine's production is halted.

A walk through the Honda plant reveals not only automation in place for today but also what's being added weekly for the future. Here's a robot—decorated to resemble Big Bird—spraying adhesive on a dashboard, a process that only one month ago was done by hand. Nearby stands a machine picking up windshields and laying them in place, a job done by two humans a few days earlier.

Honda last year spent 4% of its sales on R&D, while American Motors—Jeep's parent—spent 1%.

At both Honda and Jeep, relative levels of investment are not only a question of available capital but, perhaps even more important, of the attitudes of the workers themselves. At Jeep a management frustrated by union intransigence regards such investment skeptically. After all, why continue to upgrade a plant if union work rules frustrate cost savings?

By contrast, at Honda workers are persuaded that automation will not eliminate jobs but improve quality control, with the result that workers see it as an investment in their own job security. Thus, many new automation ideas at Honda come right from the factory floor.

With management and labor so tightly knit at Honda, the United Auto Workers hasn't been able even to come close to getting its foot in the factory door, despite continued efforts. Honda management has reason to be thankful. Consider the work rules and job classifications at Jeep. For example, the UAW contract calls for three workers, each with a different union job classification, to move parts to the assembly line. At Honda one person moves parts from inventory to line, where assembly workers pull them up as needed.

But there is more to Honda's success than automation and flexible work rules. What bonds the company together and helps generate its growth is a kind of corporate chemistry—an environment that encourages both labor and management at the firm to regard themselves collectively as "us" rather than as "us versus them."

Listen to Gary Smith, 21, a "team leader" (equivalent of a foreman) on the Honda assembly line. In between dashing back and forth to the line to help out (which isn't permitted under Jeep's *union* work rules), Smith talked with *Forbes* about life at Honda. Does he think highly profitable Honda could pay him more?

"Sure, I suppose we could demand more money right now," Smith replies," and take a chance that we'd be out of work in ten years. But I'm making straight pay of more than $12 an hour. That's three times what I made before at my dad's grocery store in Bellefontaine. I've got my car paid for and just bought a house. I've got all the money I really need. I'd rather see us reinvest than pay it all out. Job security is important to me." This is not a Japanese worker talking. This is a young midwestern American.

Employee attitudes are clearly in evidence in the differing rates of absenteeism at the two plants. On one balmy spring Friday several weeks ago, the beckoning weekend proved so alluring at Jeep that 15% of the plant's second shift, beginning at 4:30 p.m., failed to show for work, forcing management to shut the plant and send the other 85% home, without pay. The absenteeism and the attitudes it represents are probably responsible for the high number of manufacturing defects that give the Jeep a relatively low rating in *Consumer Reports'* "Frequency of Repair" surveys.

The same day Jeep shut down because of absenteeism, Honda showed an absentee rate of about 2%—typical for the firm. "Good people will show up, bonus or not," says a Jeep labor relations manager, skeptical of Honda's practice of paying attendance bonuses to employees.

He may be half right. It's good people plus good attitudes. At Honda, when asked why he and his associates had such impressive attendance figures, one worker replied matter-of-factly: "Because we want to look good for promotion."

Jeep workers, threatened with layoffs, aren't worried about "looking good" for a potential promotion. They're worried about keeping their jobs, and they think that hanging tough is the way to do it.

Nor have past AMC managements covered themselves with glory. It was they, after all, who permitted labor relations to get as bad as they did. A member of that management told us: "The union merely exists to protect guys who try to screw the company." Even if that is true, the statement betrays an attitude that bodes ill for employee morale. These were managements, after all, that lost money in five of the last six years and were recently savaged by AMC's own dealers in a survey conducted by the National Automobile Dealers Association.

Honda, by contrast, seems a beehive of camaraderie and fellow-feeling, and the company goes to great lengths to encourage it. All Honda employees, top to bottom, refer to each other as "associates." All wear white coveralls—no neckties—with first names stitched above the pocket. There are no enclosed offices, no reserved parking spaces, no executive dining rooms or lounges. In short, democratic.

As Honda's approach has worked, and its profits have risen, the company has increased hourly wages and added paid holidays, which now roughly equal those of union shops. Insurance is fully paid. Attendance bonuses and profit sharing have been added. Had these final two features been in place last year, total cash compensation at Honda for an assembly line worker with two years' tenure and perfect attendance would have been $13.58 an hour, or $28,249 annually. Those are hardly scab wages in central Ohio, where three-bedroom homes list for around $75,000.

Here, then, is perhaps as good a place as any to end our tale of two factories. One, Honda, has begun with huge advantages: a greenfield factory built from scratch, managed with a nonconfrontational attitude toward employee relations—"us" instead of "us versus them"—in pursuit of a common goal: to produce good cars economically.

Result? Honda's shareholders have seen their stock rise 220% in the last 6½ years. In the same period starting wages on the factory floor have risen 78%, not counting bonuses. And Honda of America is still building, still hiring.

At Jeep, management has failed to improve on a bad situation, which is growing worse with each passing month. As for the union, charged with protecting its members' jobs, it is actually doing the opposite, leaving management no choice but to move production elsewhere.

And here's the irony: After years of producing cars that didn't sell well, in its current line of Jeeps AMC finally has a vehicle whose ruggedness and versatility is ideally suited to one of the best segments of the U.S. auto market. What a travesty if this excellent product should founder in a sea of animosity.

SHAKING UP DETROIT[2]

American firms learn fastest not through reading books or gathering intelligence overseas but by being directly confronted with a competitor performing at a much higher level using American employees in America.

> —*Made in America: Regaining the Productive Edge*,
> MIT Commission on Industrial Productivity

Amid cornfields southeast of Lafayette, Ind., young Hoosiers are building the Subaru Legacy in a brand-new factory. Workers fresh off the farms are assembling Toyota Camrys in Georgetown, Ky., where men in bib overalls chat on the courthouse steps. In the tiny village of East Liberty, Ohio, newly hired trainees are learning to build Honda Civics at the most recent addition to Honda's manufacturing complex in nearby Marysville.

Here lies America's industrial battleground of the 1990s. In these and other semirural towns of the Midwest and Canada, Japanese carmakers have set up 10 plants, including some of the most efficient, most automated, and least unionized auto plants in North America. With superb planning and a synergistic mixture of technology and productive labor, the Japanese intend to slice a giant chunk out of the Big Three's U.S. and Canadian mar-

---

[2]Reprint of an article by James B. Treece, *Business Week* staffwriter. Reprinted from August 14, 1989 issue of *Business Week* by special permission, copyright © 1989 by McGraw-Hill, Inc.

kets. So far, they're beating the Americans on their own turf. The Big Three will suffer most from transplant production. DRI/McGraw-Hill predicts that every three autos made by the transplants will displace one import—and two Detroit entrants.

The Japanese invasion represents a great deal more than a marketing problem for General Motors, Ford, and Chrysler. It's penetrating the very heart of the domestic industry, challenging managerial mindsets and traditional, often obsolete, relations between producers and suppliers, management and labor. Since the turn of the century, Detroit auto makers have run the entire production show. Detroit dictated the industry's auto-making technology, developed a labor-relations strategy, and drew into its orbit thousands of suppliers dedicated to stamping, welding, and forging metal. If you thought cars, you thought Detroit.

Chrysler Cuts

No longer. The signs that Detroit must embrace radical reforms are compelling. Since the 1940s, the Big Three and the United Auto Workers have lived together fairly comfortably in an industrywide culture of adversary bargaining. But on July 26, workers at Nissan Motor Manufacturing Corp.'s plant in Smyrna, Tenn., rejected the union by more than a 2-to-1 vote. The overwhelming margin of victory for Nissan's antiunion management signaled the arrival of a competitive, nonunion culture that strongly threatens the UAW's grip on auto production in the U.S.

On July 27, Chrysler Chairman Lee A. Iacocca announced plans to cut 2,300 white-collar workers as part of a $1 billion belt-tightening package. This is only a forerunner of what's to come. The Japanese transplants' compacts, sporty cars, and trucks are targeted at segments where Chrysler is most dependent for sales. Iacocca also doubled Chrysler's rebates on cars, and Ford Motor Co. responded on Aug. 1 with rebates of at least $1,000 on every Lincoln and Mercury car it sells.

General Motors Corp., which is operating only at 75% to 80% of capacity, is even more vulnerable than Chrysler and Ford. Auto analysts say it must phase out the equivalent of four assembly plants. "The competition is going to be fierce," warns GM President Robert C. Stempel. "If you thought it was tough this year, you ain't seen nothing yet."

Stempel was referring to a long-gathering overcapacity problem that now looms directly over Detroit. With six new plants opening in the past year alone, the transplants have significantly increased the supply of cars and trucks in the North American market. U.S. capacity next year will exceed demand by 2.7 million vehicles—and the surplus could rise above 3 million by 1994. Ignoring the current sales slump, the Japanese plan to boost U.S. production 41% in the fourth quarter, even as General Motors, Ford, and Chrysler cut their output by 18%. Indeed, in the first half of 1989, Japanese transplants built 14.7% of the passenger cars produced in the U.S., up from 8.9% only two years ago. In addition, Korea's Hyundai Motor Co. soon will be producing 100,000 cars a year in Quebec.

Midwest Gains

The new factories will enable the Asian auto companies to boost sales regardless of quotas, tariffs, or currency swings. Take this year: Japanese car imports were off 3.6% in the first six months. But surging transplant production has pushed sales of popular Japanese nameplates up 5.5% in a weak market. Much of the gain is in the Midwestern states, traditionally Detroit strongholds, but now home of the transplants.

It wasn't supposed to work this way. When the Big Three and the UAW pressured the Japanese early in the 1980s to build cars in America with union labor, management and labor assumed they would quickly create a level playing field. Forced to pay UAW wages and accept Big Three work practices, the transplants would lose the cost advantage of producing in Japan. The Big Three "thought poor quality and high absenteeism were part and parcel of doing business here," says Maryann Keller, an auto analyst at Furman Selz Mager Dietz & Birney Inc. But the Japanese weren't about to play by American rules.

Gerrymandering

With only a few exceptions, Japanese auto makers, aided by fat state subsidies, built their plants in semirural areas of the Midwest. They hired mostly young workers with little industrial experience—and no love of unionism. As a result, the transplants enjoy lower health care costs and less costly pension liabilities.

But some Japanese companies have come under attack for hiring relatively few blacks. In 1988, Honda Motor Co. paid $6 million to about 370 blacks and women as a result of job discrimination charges brought by the Equal Employment Opportunity Commission. While giving hiring preference to residents in the Marysville area, the EEOC said, Honda gerrymandered the map to exclude nearby Columbus and its large black population.

Other transplants may have used similar practices. Two University of Michigan professors studied hiring at plants built in the same period by Japanese and Big Three companies. Compared with the Big Three, the Japanese tended not only to choose areas with low percentages of racial minorities but also to hire fewer blacks from the regional labor pool.

Only three of seven transplants in the U.S. are unionized—and those only because they're linked with the Big Three companies. They are New United Motor Manufacturing (NUMMI), in Fremont, Calif.; Diamond-Star Motors in Normal, Ill.; and Mazda Motor Manufacturing (USA) in Flat Rock, Mich. Even at these plants, UAW pacts allow managers to deploy workers in a much more flexible, less costly way than they do at many Big Three plants.

Quality Control

The transplants also import a large part of their auto components from Japan or buy from nonunion Japanese suppliers who have relocated in the U.S. They are thus able to control prices and quality. As a result of these and other practices, the transplants enjoy a $700-per-vehicle cost advantage over Big Three plants, or about one-tenth the retail cost of a small car, says Candice Howes, a UAW economist.

Hoping to reduce this gap, Detroit is being forced to learn from the transplants how to improve efficiency and quality. Although powerful forces within the industry are resisting change, the Big Three are slowly diassembling management and production methods and are remaking them along Japanese lines. Companies that had nearly given up on American workers are finding that giving them decision-making power can be a powerful motivator. U.S. parts makers are learning humbling lessons in quality and cost-cutting as the Japanese plants reject parts that had been good enough for Detroit.

Japan and the U.S.

Indeed, the entire producer-supplier relatio[...]
Three was ripe for drastic change. Traditionally,[...]
auto makers have dealt with suppliers at arm's leng[...]
vendors mainly on the basis of price competition. The[...]
however, form long-term, close relationships with suppl[...]

Carmakers share information and strategic goals wit[...]
vendors, help them to improve quality, and jointly develop [...]
technology and training programs for workers. In the U.S., say[...]
Fujio Cho, executive vice-president and chief operating officer at
Toyota Motor Manufacturing USA Inc. in Kentucky, "we've
been trying to establish good long-term relations and avoid relations where you buy when it's cheap and say goodbye when it's
expensive."

Such a different philosophy produced traumas when U.S.
suppliers first tried to sell to the transplants. For example, the
Japanese emphasize cost-cutting. In the U.S., notes David M.
Merchant, a former manager at Mazda's Michigan plant, if a part
cost $1 the first year, both supplier and buyer assumed it would
cost $1.10 the next year because of inflation. But the Japanese ex-
pect the cost to drop to 90¢ because of improvements in costs and
quality. When Mazda's suppliers ran into this attitude, Merchant
says, "it was kind of a shock." Under conventional U.S. practices,
he adds, "the supplier community has produced a lot of
multimillionaires."

Quality was the big stumbling block for American suppliers
in the early transplant years. Parts makers soon discovered that
the transplant producers expected them to adjust to Japanese
standards. In quality tests, not only the part but the process by
which it's made is inspected—along with the company's books.
That method used to annoy suppliers, but they've mellowed as
the Big Three—copying the Japanese—also began to send scout-
ing parties to suppliers' plants. Toshikata Amino, executive vice-
president of Honda of America Mfg. Inc., remembers how puz-
zled U.S. component manufacturers were when Honda opened
a motorcycle plant in Marysville, Ohio, in 1976. "The industry's
understanding of the Japanese ways of doing business was
superficial," he says. Since then, he adds, suppliers have deepened
their knowledge. "I see some domino effect," he says.

Lessons

e Japanese still don't buy much
hat annoys U.S. companies. The
cars have local content of 60%
mula that includes advertising
study by the General Account-
8 average domestic content at
e. That difference cost Ameri-
O estimates.

...sprants' loyalty to their long-term Japanese suppliers
hasn't gone unnoticed in Detroit. All of the Big Three, but Ford
in particular, have learned that such loyalty encourages suppliers
to spend more on research and development. The U.S. companies are absorbing lessons like this mainly by sending their own
people to work in a transplant that they jointly own. The man-
date: Return and promote change. "If we can open up minds and
break down these not-invented-here attitudes, that's the greatest
thing we can get from this kind of a venture," says Chrysler's Iacocca.

To speed up the transfer of ideas from its joint venture with
Mitsubishi Motor Corp. at Diamond-Star, Chrysler assigned a
company plane to make a weekly Tuesday shuttle from Detroit
to Normal, Ill. At General Motors, though, absorbing the lessons
of NUMMI was more difficult. GM wasn't looking for what it
found. The company wanted to learn Toyota's management
methods but assumed those would focus on managing technology. The central lessons, however, went much deeper, involving
GM's bureaucratic management style. For GM to adopt NUMMI-
like ways will require a major overhaul of the company's values.

In GM's culture, it was unacceptable to publicly admit having
a problem. The first GM executives assigned to NUMMI under
Toyota managers took nearly six months to realize that the Japanese wanted problems exposed and fixed, not hidden. This gave
them something to work on jointly with the Americans. Gary D.
Kowalski, now director of logistics and administration at GM's
Truck & Bus Group, can still recall the day his Japanese boss
looked him in the eye and said: "No problem is a problem."

Stephen L. Bera loved his work as a raw-materials manager
at NUMMI. After being chided for raising his voice to subordi-
nates, "I mellowed out," he says. He absorbed the Toyota philoso-

phy, which bans time clocks, for instance, on the grounds that trust is not gained but lost. Then, two years into his three-year NUMMI stint, he asked were GM planned to place him upon return to the corporation. There was no plan. He quit, believing that General Motors wasn't ready to absorb NUMMI's lessons.

The company took more care in placing the second crew of returnees from NUMMI. "We've all been assigned positions where we can have a fairly significant impact on the operations of the business," says Mark T. Hogan, now group director of business planning at GM's Truck & Bus Group. "You can look at us as kind of like missionaries or apostles," he says. His gospel: "The importance of job security in getting and keeping the dedication of the work force."

American unions have been saying this for years, but the example of the transplants is bolstering their argument. A no-layoff policy covering hourly workers is one of the key elements of Japanese labor and production systems. Others include continual training, participation in shop-floor decision-making, team-based production, and group bonus or profit-sharing plans. All of these have been used sparingly by U.S. companies, but the Japanese make it a point to combine them in a comprehensive system that aims at gaining the loyalty of employees and binding them to the company.

The transplants' no-layoff policies have certainly done that. After Nissan's Sentra hit a sales slump in 1988, the Smyrna plant kept producing cars, parking them in a nearby cow pasture. Nissan was not bound by union contract to avoid layoffs, but the policy undoubtedly aided the company in defeating the UAW. Meanwhile, UAW contracts at NUMMI and Mazda in Flat Rock allow layoffs only if economic conditions are so severe "that the company's long-term financial viability is threatened." When sales of the Chevrolet Nova, produced by NUMMI, dropped last year, the company assigned surplus workers to training programs and prepared for the launch of the Nova's replacement, Chevy's Geo Prizm. Not only did they keep their jobs, but they welcomed the chance to get extra training.

NUMMI's willingness to sign a no-layoff provision and give the union a role in decision-making impressed George Nano, the UAW's bargaining committee chairman at the plant. "People make cars," he says. "Technology doesn't make cars. I doubt everyone at GM agrees with that."

Lino J. Piedra, chairman of Diamond-Star, makes a similar point. His plant, crammed with robots, is the world's most technologically advanced assembly plant, says the National Society of Professional Engineers. But Piedra doesn't see technology alone as the competitive edge. "The people working here have a sensitivity to working together. That's the important thing to me," he says. "Anybody can buy a robot."

Respect for employees is a consistent theme at the transplants. Management carefully selects job applicants, trains them thoroughly and often, and treats them with dignity and trust. The approach has yielded highly motivated, involved workers.

A willingness to work in a team environment is far more important than experience in the selection process. At Flat Rock, just south of Detroit, 80% of Mazda's employees have no automotive experience at all—by management choice. "They haven't been exposed to the traditional ills of the auto world," says James F. Korowin, vice-president of operations. "They're open to learning." Adds Sam D. Heltman, general manager of human resources at Toyota's Georgetown plant: "I'm already seeing other companies looking at more thorough selection systems and taking the time to decide what kind of people you want in the work force."

'Life-Long Learning'

At Subaru-Isuzu Automotive Inc., job applicants must have a high school diploma or equivalent. Grades don't matter, only finishing the course work does, because it shows a commitment to education. "From Day One here, the emphasis is on life-long learning," says Tim Miller, who trains newly hired workers. "A person is not going to learn a job and then do it the rest of their life." Typically, a job candidate at a transplant goes through a series of tests and interviews before being hired.

The transplants are by no means without blemishes. Despite all the effort to build goodwill, part of the transplants' work force is dissatisfied. Last June, NUMMI workers elected slightly more hard-line candidates to four of eight slots on the UAW's shop committee, and Mazda's local voted out officers who were seen as too cozy with management. Nearly one-third of Nissan's Smyrna workers voted for representation by the UAW, partly because of health problems stemming from what the critics call "speedup."

Fast Pace

It's not so much that the transplants' assembly lines run faster than the Big Three's. Rather, the Japanese insist on a higher work intensity. They use the *kaizen* concept that calls for assemblers to make continuous improvements in performing their tasks, both to improve quality and to eliminate unneeded motion. There is continuing pressure to produce cars at the same line speed with fewer people. Harley Shaiken, a professor at the University of California at San Diego, says that at GM's modern Linden (N.J.) plant, workers work 48 seconds out of every minute. At NUMMI, they work 55 seconds a minute.

Isamu Nobuto, president of Mazda's Flat Rock plant, doesn't deny that workers have little free time. "People should be employed doing work that has value. It is not respecting the employee if we have them doing work that is wasteful." But it's hard to transfer this concept to Big Three plants, where labor and management have long considered themselves on opposite sides of a chasm. In this climate, veteran assembly line workers question whether working harder serves their interests as well as management's. Staunch unionists also worry about other Japanese practices, such as discouraging workers from filing grievances. This weakens the union's basic role as a grievance processor. And lumping all production workers into one job classification and basing promotions on merit undermine the bedrock principle of seniority.

But change seems unavoidable, for both labor and management. There's no shortage of Americans wanting to buy Japanese cars or willing to work for Japanese employers. U.S. auto makers must apply the lessons they learn from the transplants. If they don't their place will be taken by another U.S. carmaker—with a Japanese name.

U.S., JAPAN REACH TRUCE IN CHIPS WAR[3]

The trade war over silicon chips reached a truce at midnight on 31 July, the last possible moment before a deadline set by the United States.

This marked the end of hostilities between U.S. and Japanese makers of semiconductors, carriers of the minute circuits that lie at the heart of modern electronics. The struggle raged in the courts and conference rooms for a year, sparked by complaints that Japan was breaking fair-trade laws.

Had the deadline passed without agreement, the United States intended to put back into effect some stiff fees levied on importers of Japanese chips earlier this year. The fines, covering several advanced memory chips, were suspended while the government awaited the outcome of these talks.

The carrot-and-stick approach seems to have worked. U.S. officials say that the volume of U.S. chip sales in Japan may double in the next 5 years, increasing from around $800 million to $2 billion.

The U.S. companies accused the Japanese of two trade violations: limiting the sale of U.S. chips in Japan and promoting the sale of Japanese chips in the United States through unfair price competition. The American companies asked the government for help on the ground that the United States must have a healthy chip industry if it wants a healthy electronics industry. National security was invoked as well, in that the effectiveness of U.S. weapons rests on the quality of their electronic parts. Government officials found the case persuasive. In winning this agreement, they claim to have saved a vital high-technology industry.

The text of the agreement has not been published. However, it seems to be one-sided, consisting mainly of Japanese promises to buy more U.S. chips and to avoid extreme price-cutting. The Americans simply agreed not to impose the threatened duties, provided Japan keeps its end of the bargain. There are no numerical goals or timetables, but secret "side letters" apparently call for

[3]Reprint of an article by Eliot Marshall, *Science* staffwriter. Reprinted by permission from *Science*, August 15, 1986. Copyright © 1986 by the American Association for the Advancement of Science.

U.S. chip sales in Japan to grow steadily through 1991. The measure of Japanese cooperation, a Commerce Department official said, will be "the sound of cash registers ringing."

The Japanese Ministry of International Trade and Industry (MITI) pledged to help change the pattern of trade in several ways. It will create a new organization to act as a liaison between U.S. sellers and Japanese buyers. This outfit will collect and publish data on foreign products, hold seminars, and organize research fellowships for foreigners in Japan. MITI also will invite American companies into joint ventures with Japanese manufacturers to develop new products. Finally, the Japanese government has pledged to collect data on domestic chip manufacturing, exporting, and pricing, and to share the data quickly with U.S. officials if and when new trade complaints arise.

President Reagan praised Commerce Secretary Malcolm Baldridge and Special Trade Representative Clayton Yeutter for hammering out "an historic agreement." George Scalise, head of the public policy committee for the Semiconductor Industry Association, spoke with no great modesty of his own industry as the "most important basic industry for the rest of this century," saying the pact opened "a new era in trade relations" with Japan.

Behind the scenes, however, experts remained skeptical about the long-term value of the agreement. For industry, the main concern is that the pact may not be enforced. "We've been burned before," said SIA economist Steven Benz, speaking of Japan's promises in the 1970's to open its market to U.S. electronic products. The immediate effect will be to boost the U.S. companies' stocks and raise the prices of some chips. The Japanese were accused of "dumping" certain products. (To dump is to sell below the cost of manufacture plus profit. Cost and profit are defined by the U.S. International Trade Commission.) The Japanese denied that they engaged in dumping, but nevertheless agreed to stop, and so prices will go up. "It is a decent agreement," Benz said, "But given past history, we will have to wait to see whether it provides substantial help."

Nonindustry observers had other doubts. For example, one federal official at work on a study of chip manufacturing said, "This isn't going to transform the American semiconductor industry; it won't end the internal problems." He argues that the Japanese are successful because they have developed better manufacturing technologies, not because they violate trade rules.

"What is dumping?" he asks. "It's just an emotional term." In his view, Japan leads the world in the quality of semiconductor fabrication and production processes. "It's no longer 1971. The managers who are screaming about the Japanese are the ones who built up these companies in the 1970's. They don't realize that things have changed."

A new study of the semiconductor market at the National Science Foundation supports the view that domestic problems may afflict the industry more than competition from Japan. This came to light as researchers worked on a two-part review of the threat to national security posed by imported silicon chips (*Science*, 4 April, p. 12). The President's National Security Council is coordinating one part and the Defense Science Board (DSB) at the Pentagon is running the other. NSF has taken a hand in drafting the security council study.

Researchers scoured the data banks for the latest and best information and were surprised by what they found. If the numbers prove correct, Japanese competition is not the only—or the primary—cause of distress. The turmoil may be due to a general market shuffle in which big companies are pushing out small ones. Thus, under the new trade pact, Japan may be penalized for problems not entirely of its making.

Market analysts divide the chip business into three categories: (1) the importers, (ii) the relatively small companies that specialize in making chips, called "merchants," and (iii) the chip-making subdivisions of much bigger corporations, known as the "captives." Typical merchants are Intel, National Semiconductor, and Advanced Micro Devices. Two major captives are the semiconductor divisions of AT&T and IBM.

According to one NSF expert, "The quality and consistency of the data we've seen are not good, but a significant point has come out. It looks as though the U.S. merchants have lost more to U.S. captives than to the Japanese." The captives have been growing slowly but steadily over the last decade, while the merchants have moved in irregular ups and downs. These smaller merchant companies are severely affected by the peaks and dips in demand, living a marginal kind of existence that makes it difficult to invest adequately in new R&D. The captives now appear to control 45 to 50 percent of the U.S. market. However, the researcher warned that the number are weak, because it is nearly as hard to get information on the secretive U.S. captive companies as to learn about the Soviet chip market.

A similarly bleak analysis appeared in a recent paper by MIT political scientist Charles Ferguson, titled "American Microelectronics in Decline." He wrote that the U.S. industry is "substantially inferior to Japan's in most product and process technologies" because it has never reorganized to meet the new global competition. Instead, it remains "highly vulnerable, fragmented, and poorly suited to intense competition. . . . " Protectionist measures will not help, Ferguson claims, unless they are accompanied by a compaign to restructure the industry.

Ferguson spoke before the Defense Science Board's Task Force on Semiconductor Dependency earlier this year, and the group may have taken his comments to heart. In any case, it has decided to look into the industry's structural problems as well as the military's particular concern for a secure source of supply. Both this DSB report and the National Security Council study are being thoroughly rewritten to take account of new data and provide a broader perspective on industry problems. Along with a third report on semiconductors at the National Academy of Engineering, they are scheduled for release in September.

One controversial proposal the DSB may offer in the line of structural reform is that the Pentagon invest in a new "chip foundry." The idea may follow the Japanese model, calling for a large federal subsidy (perhaps $200 million a year for 5 years), but leaving management strictly in private hands. The exact purpose of the foundry has not been settled. In one scheme it would serve as an R&D center for testing new approaches to manufacturing; in another, it would be a shared factory to produce chips designed elsewhere; and in a third, it would serve as a mass production center for advanced memory chips. There are problems with each suggestion, not the least of them political. The Pentagon may not have room in its budget for anything so grandiose.

Meanwhile, Charles Sporck, president of the National Semiconductor Corporation, is trying to interest his peers in another joint manufacturing idea. Interviewed in July by *Electronic News*, he said his efforts were just in the "early stages" and that he was trying to learn if there was any consensus for a joint venture in the industry. He spoke of the need for "an overall integrated development plan" that would enable U.S. companies to compete with Japan by coordinating their manufacturing investments. In the past, he said, the chip makers had been too "fragmented" in their demands on companies that design production machinery.

He mentioned no definite proposal but said, "There will have to be government funding in some way."

On 31 July, the government won at least the promise of respite from Japanese competition in the silicon chip trade. It remains to be seen how the U.S. industry will use the breathing spell.

TRADE FACE-OFF[4]

It is no larger than a few grains of rice, but it was big enough to cause one of the most serious episodes between the U.S. and Japan since the end of World War II. It is the tiny microchip, a sophisticated bit of silicon that is the indispensable heart of the techtronic age, the raw material for everything from talking teddy bears to personal computers to intercontinental missiles. After the Reagan Administration imposed trade sanctions against Japan in an attempt to protect American makers of microchips, it suddenly looked last week as if the U.S. and Japan were headed for what could become a major trade row. In fact, Tokyo TV commentators described the event with the phrase *Kaisen zen-ya* (the eve of war), an expression used to describe the days before Pearl Harbor. In Washington, U.S. Trade Representative Clayton Yeutter, while insisting that a trade war was not at hand, nonetheless called the confrontation a "serious dispute."

Sizable shock waves rattled around the world in the wake of the U.S. action, which was prompted by alleged Japanese cheating in the sale of the useful semiconductors and by Tokyo's alleged intransigent protection of its domestic microchip market. Partially in response to the specter of trade confrontation, the Dow Jones average of 30 industrial stocks sank 57.39 points as the week began, its third worst plunge in history. Yet the amazing 4½-year bull market in stocks, fueled in part by billions of dollars in Japanese investment money, recovered quickly, and the Dow closed the week at 2390.34, a record. In Tokyo money markets, the price of the U.S. dollar slumped to a doleful 144.7 yen, the

[4]Reprint of an article by George Russell, *Time* staffwriter. Reprinted by permission from *Time*, April 13, 1987. Copyright © 1987 Time Inc.

first time in postwar history that the greenback was worth less
than 145. Only 15 months ago it was 200. As tempers cooled by
the end of the week, however, the dollar had climbed back to
146.05.

In both the U.S. and Japan, the Administration's tough action
sparked widespread consternation. Japan's largest daily, *Yomiuri
Shimbun*, editorialized that the sanctions were "detrimental to the
interests of American consumers." The liberal daily *Asahi
Shimbun* declared darkly that "trade war has now come about." In
Manhattan, the usually pro-Reaganaut *Wall Street Journal* warned
that "high-stakes trade retaliation, like Russian roulette, is a dangerous game, and the world doesn't benefit when the President
of the United States leads by bad example."

Japanese officials rushed to keep the trade conflict from spin-
ning out of control. Foreign Minister Tadashi Kuranari urged
that "overall U.S.-Japanese relations should not be undermined
by this issue." Makoto Kuroda, a senior member of the country's
powerful Ministry of International Trade and Industry (MITI),
prepared to hie to Washington. His job: to convey dismay at the
bombshell U.S. decision to retaliate with some $300 million
worth of tariffs on a wide range of Japanese electronic goods. In
addition, former Japanese Foreign Minister Shintaro Abe has
been named as a special envoy by Tokyo to help deflect the trade
collision. But the sanctions will almost certainly go into effect as
scheduled on or about April 17.

The measures amounted to little more than a blip on the gar-
gantuan volume of annual U.S.-Japanese trade, which totaled
$112 billion last year. But the slap at Tokyo was also a powerful
diplomatic message. For the first time, longstanding American
grievances over the trade practices of its second largest trading
partner (after Canada) had resulted in a sharp and pointed U.S.
economic response. Said a senior Administration official: "This
will hopefully send a signal to all our trading partners that the
free ride is over." As Commerce Secretary Malcolm Baldrige put
it to *Time*, "You can't rely on words. You have to rely on actions."

Those actions may soon provide some trying moments for
two men widely touted as close personal and political friends:
Ronald Reagan and Japanese Prime Minister Yasuhiro Nakasone.
The two statesmen are scheduled to meet in Washington on April
29, and the new strain in their relationship comes at a time when
both leaders face serious political troubles. At home Nakasone is

currently fighting an uphill battle for political survival. The U.S. sanctions were an added burden that could help force him out of office before his term expires in October.

For Reagan, weakened by the Iranscam scandal, the sanctions were an unprecedented gamble. On one hand, they expressed the Administration's "profound disapproval" of Japanese trading practices in the sensitive semiconductor field. On the other, they were an integral part of the Administration's strategy to address the country's ghastly trade deficit. The semiconductor measures were also intended, ironically enough, to help block a rising protectionist tide in the U.S. Congress, but they could just as easily have the opposite effect.

The sanctions actually cheered legislators who are preparing a new version of a tough omnibus trade bill that passed the House of Representatives last year but died in the Senate. One version of the new bill is expected to reach the House floor on April 28, the day before Nakasone's visit. Says Senator Max Baucus of Montana, a leading congressional activist on trade issues: "The President's semiconductor action is sort of a turning point. We're going to stop talking and start taking action."

The clash over microchips also went far beyond commercial concerns in pitting two vastly different cultures against each other. After more than 130 years of contact with the West, Japan is hardworking, thrifty, highly organized but still relatively insular in its world view. On the other hand, free-wheeling, free-spending and individualistic America is now becoming fully aware of the loss of its postwar industrial primacy. By its latest trade actions, Washington was clearly attempting to force Tokyo to change not only its outlook but also its historic attitudes. For the Reagan Administration, and indeed for America, the issue of protecting high-tech industries went beyond economics and politics to national pride. Long the world's technological leader— and still in many respects the world front runner—the U.S. was fighting hard to protect that role.

The semiconductor fray, predicts Clyde Prestowitz, an expert on Japan at Washington's Woodrow Wilson International Center for Scholars, "is probably just the beginning of much more rocky times between the U.S. and Japan." Or between Japan and just about everybody else. In London last week the Conservative Cabinet of British Prime Minister Margaret Thatcher closeted itself to discuss economic measures against the Pacific island power. After the hour-long session at 10 Downing Street, Thatcher dispatched one of her trade ministers to Japan with the threat that Britain might soon take retaliatory action to keep additional Japanese banks and securities firms from operating in London. The aim was to pressure Tokyo into ending its stonewalling of British firms that want access to highly protected Japanese financial markets.

The British have urged their eleven fellow members of the European Community to take part in the Japanese sanctions campaign, and several E.C. members seem inclined to join in. Said European Community Industrial Commissioner Karl-Heinz Narjes: "Our patience has snapped. We have had enough of giving the Japanese the benefit of the doubt." At a meeting of Community foreign ministers scheduled to take place last weekend, the Netherlands and West Germany were expected to support the British proposal. Last month in Brussels the European Commission urged Community members to get tough with Japan. The commission had earlier slapped a 20% retaliatory tariff on Japanese photocopying machines, which take up 75% of the $1 billion European market.

Behind the sound and fury aimed at Japan were profound alterations in the familiar international economic landscape that will continue to shake trading relationships for years to come. An unwholesome tide of global protectionism, has been slowly rising for several years, but now it seems to be heading toward flood levels. That unsettling prospect comes despite the avowed intention of most of the world's trading nations to broaden free trade through a new round of negotiations involving the 96-member General Agreement on Tariffs and Trade. Even though talks for that round began in Uruguay last September, the Geneva-based staff of GATT is deeply concerned about the outcome. In its latest annual report, issued last December, the organization declared that economic policies being introduced around the world might not lead to open trade warfare but could produce a "prolonged stagnation."

Free trade has been a central tenet of the postwar economic order. The system that was put in place with U.S. leadership took as a cardinal principle the belief that "beggar-thy-neighbor" protectionism in the prewar years had helped cause the Depression-era misery and social turbulence that eventually led to World War

II. In economic terms, protectionist barriers largely benefit inefficient companies and hurt consumers by forcing them to pay more for products. Even though the competition engendered by free trade can cause temporary pain by destroying obsolete industry and generating unemployment, the final result is more jobs, more income and more opportunity if every manufacturer is allowed to produce and export what it makes best. The value of free trade has been spectacularly displayed in the tremendous expansion of postwar Western wealth.

Protectionists, on the other hand, argue that free trade is a fine theory but it is not the real world. They claim that at any given time trading nations are subsidizing production costs, stopping imports by stealth and off-loading their own products on less sheltered trading partners. The strongest protectionist argument is that industries may need either temporary or permanent help in combatting such unfair competition, usually in the form of trade restrictions. The biggest problem with the argument is that temporary help often turns into the kind of permanent dependence that fosters stagnation.

The protectionist argument is flaring up anew because of Japan's phenomenal success. After only 30 years of aggressive, imaginative but often highly protected industrial growth, the Japanese are the prodigies of the industrialized world, reveling in a trade surplus of $83 billion in 1986 alone. Says Robert Hormats, a partner in the Goldman Sachs investment house and a former trade adviser to the Carter and Reagan Administrations: "No country in history has ever gained international wealth as fast as Japan." Many economists estimate that the accumulated Japanese balance of payments surplus could reach anywhere from $500 billion to $1 trillion by the year 2000. The Japanese, like the OPEC nations in their heyday, are already investing their current surplus funds around the world. Last year they placed $132 billion abroad, roughly half of it in U.S. Government and corporate bonds.

Japan's rise to such riches has been particularly painful for the U.S., the world's foremost military power and Tokyo's most important ally. As of last year the U.S. had also become the world's biggest foreign debtor (1986 total: more than $200 billion). That debt is steadily being compounded by the trade deficit, which rose to a new record of $169.8 billion last year. Of that total, $58.6 billion was owed to Japan, based on $85.5 billion in Japanese imports to the U.S. and only $26.9 billion worth of return U.S. exports.

The irony is that probably at no other time in postwar history have the U.S. and Japan managed to cooperate as well as they have under Reagan and Nakasone. In the past five years, the two countries have reached an unprecedented degree of understanding on Japan's strategic role in the Pacific. That Japanese contribution is, quite simply, invaluable. Says Katsuro Sakoh, a senior fellow in Asian studies at the conservative Heritage Foundation. "Security is the cornerstone of the U.S.-Japanese relationship." Japan's 1987 military budget of $32 billion is now the world's third largest after that of the U.S. and the Soviet Union. Under Nakasone, Japan is beginning to meet a long-standing but unfulfilled commitment to safeguard its own sea-lanes up to 1,000 miles off the Japanese coast.

But while the security ties have thickened, the trade imbalance has widened. It is now more than three times as great as it was only five years ago. From year to year a trade deficit may not be a bad thing, but over time it becomes debilitating, since money must be borrowed abroad to finance the shortfall. Even then, such borrowing can be useful if it is used to finance needed capital improvements, as the U.S. did in the 19th century. The current U.S. trade deficit, however, is largely a result of America's passion for more consumer goods.

Another problem is the deficit's intractability. During the past 15 years, the U.S. has had successive trade crises with the Japanese as the archipelagic powerhouse had conquered world markets in textiles, television sets, steel and automobiles. In each case, the problem was supposedly solved by the imposition of controls of Japanese exports to the U.S. But the imbalance has become worse, creating a climate—at least in Washington—that threatens to undercut the much broader mutuality of interest that binds the U.S. and Japan. Says an Administration official: "It really is a problem of perception. The Japanese are seen as being unfair."

That is not the Japanese view. As concern over the U.S. trade deficit has grown, Nakasone has taken the lead in trying to persuade his countrymen to become more energetic consumers, especially of foreign goods, in the interests of averting a trade war. The Prime Minister two years ago made an unprecedented appearance on national television to underscore that appeal. He then went on a highly publicized expedition to buy foreign goods in Tokyo. At that time he also announced relaxations in the maze of bureaucratic regulations that often seem to make the Japanese market impenetrable to foreign competition.

Nakasone's efforts at liberalization, though, have had little effect on U.S.-Japanese trade figures. Indeed, most economists estimate that if all protectionist barriers in Japan were removed at a stroke, Japanese imports would increase by only $8 billion to $15 billion.

The factor that has had the greatest single impact on Japanese trade is the skyrocketing value of the yen, which has risen 60% against the U.S. dollar since September 1985. The steep rise in the yen has helped push the Japanese economy into a trough. The change in currency value was expected to help correct the trade imbalance by making U.S. exports to Japan cheaper and Japanese exports to the U.S. more expensive. Finally, after long and frustrating delays, there are signs that such changes are slowly coming about. The Japanese claim their U.S. imports last year rose by almost 24%. When special circumstances are subtracted (notably, a $2.5 billion purchase of gold for coins commemorating Emperor Hirohito's 60 years of rule), the figure is more like 4.8%. But at the same time, global Japanese exports declined in volume by 1.3%.

There are additional reasons why the current semiconductor confrontation has more powerful significance than previous trade squabbles. One is the importance of the microchips—finely etched electronic devices that process thousands of bits of information per second—to the burgeoning world of high tech. Semiconductors are now used in virtually every advanced technology, including the Cray supercomputers that are a key component of the Reagan Administration's Strategic Defense Initiative. Says C. Fred Bergsten, director of the Washington-based Institute for International Economics: "Practically everyone in the U.S. agrees that semiconductors is a critical industry and that it would be dangerous, both to the economy and to national security, to lose it."

So far, the U.S. has lost neither its ability to produce semiconductors nor its capacity to manufacture other advanced and economically competitive high-technological goods. Last year the U.S. produced an estimated $227 billion worth of electronic products, including $580 million worth of supercomputers that are widely considered to be the world's most advanced machines.

The problem is that under the relentless technological advance of Japan, the once unquestioned U.S. dominance in those areas has been seriously eroded. In the semiconductor field, the U.S. in 1982 enjoyed a 49.1% world-market share, while Japan had 26.9%. Now Japan is the No. 1 producer, with 45.5% of the $45 billion world market, while the U.S. has 44%. In the overall area of high tech, the news for the U.S. has been even more depressing. In 1980 the U.S. ran a record $27 billion trade surplus in those advanced products. Last year, for the first time, the American high-tech balance became a deficit of $2.6 billion. Says the Woodrow Wilson Center's Prestowitz: "It used to be that we could say America should be moving into the future. Now we are finding out that we don't have a future."

That considerably overstates the case, but many others have taken even more alarmist positions. In February a high-level advisory panel, reporting to Defense Secretary Caspar Weinberger, issued a study that warned of the imminent demise of the U.S. semiconductor industry unless immediate acton was taken to save it. Among other things, the panel called on the Defense Department to invest $2 billion during the next five years in microchip research and development.

None of that concern entirely explains the fireworks that have erupted over the complicated U.S.-Japanese microchip agreement. The crisis actually began in the early 1980s, when both U.S. and Japanese semiconductor manufacturers, anticipating a substantial jump in demand, vastly increased their capacity for production of the microchips that are used in small numbers in personal computers and in much greater numbers in more complex machines. Instead came a two-year slump that drove down the price of the industry's most important item, the 256K DRAM (dynamic random access memory) chip, from nearly $40 to as little as $2. U.S. manufacturers charged that the Japanese continued to advance their market share in the field by selling the chips at less than cost, a practice known as dumping.

Under the July semiconductor pact, Tokyo agreed to abide by so-called fair market values for microchips set by the U.S. Department of Commerce. Japanese manufacturers could not undercut those prices in the U.S. market without violating American antidumping laws. Tokyo also made a commitment to prevent dumping by Japanese semiconductor producers in other, so-called third-country (non-U.S. and non-Japan) markets, and to encourage Japanese companies at home to buy more foreign-made chips, meaning, by and large, those made in the U.S.

Yet almost as soon as the agreement was signed, the U.S. began charging that it was being violated. The main culprits, in Washington's view, were Japanese manufacturers who continued to dump semiconductors, either directly or through middlemen, in such Asian markets as Hong Kong. Taiwan and Singapore. Washington was as sure of that activity "as I'm sitting here," declares Commerce Secretary Malcolm Baldrige. In January the Reagan Administration privately warned Japan that some kind of retaliation was likely unless the practice stopped. Washington finally conducted an investigation and satisfied itself that dumping had taken place. The Administration's preliminary finding is that there has also been no increase in Japanese purchases of foreign microchips.

Finally, the day before President Reagan announced the sanctions, the decision was endorsed by the White House's twelve-member Economic Policy Council, a Cabinet-level body chaired either by the President or, in his absence, by Treasury Secretary James Baker. With Baker in charge, the council fretted considerably over its decision. According to one Administration insider, there were sharply differing views about the value of the semiconductor agreement in the first place. Nonetheless, the group reluctantly agreed to go ahead with retaliation.

Much about the semiconductor pact is indeed questionable in economic terms. Among other things, it raises the costs of American manufacturers who use the devices to build computers and other products, thus making them more vulnerable to foreign competition. But to U.S. trade officials, the evidence of alleged Japanese dumping and Japan's refusal to open domestic semiconductor markets were the last straw. For one thing, the ink on the semiconductor agreement was barely dry before, in Washington's view, it was being ignored. For another, that Japanese behavior seemed to U.S. officials to be part of a familiar Japanese attitude toward trade issues: delay followed by nominal agreement followed by intransigence.

The American list of similar complaints on that score is long. In the past ten years, Washington has pressed mightily to open Japanese markets to such exports as beef, oranges and even U.S.-made baseball bats for a baseball-mad country. In almost all those situations, the U.S. has eventually succeeded, at least to some ex-

tent. Last October, for example, Japan agreed to open its cigarette market to U.S. manufacturers by suspending its 20% tariff
on that product. American cigarette manufacturers estimate that
their market in Japan will quintuple, to an estimated $1 billion
annually. But in every such case, contends an Administration official, "we have had to land the full power and majesty of the Government on the Japanese. Every single thing is a fight that gets
up almost to the Cabinet level."

Adding to the frustration is a backlog of other trade irritants
that could continue to flare up. One is Japanese reluctance to allow U.S. bidders to compete for a slice of the country's premier
construction project, the $6.5 billion Kansai international airport
now under construction near Osaka. Another is the longstanding American complaint that the Japanese have not been
buying enough U.S. auto parts. Particularly galling to the U.S.
was a statement attributed to MITI Official Kuroda to the effect
that American supercomputer manufacturers were wasting their
time trying to sell the advanced machines to the Japanese government and universities. So far, Minneapolis-based Cray Research
has managed to sell only seven of its supercomputing systems
(cost: $2.5 million to $16 million each) in Japan over the past
eight years. All but one of the sales were to private Japanese companies.

According to Commerce Secretary Baldrige, the new U.S.
sanctions ensure that there will now be a "different bargaining atmosphere in the future" and, he added, a "much healthier one."
Whether that proves to be true, some Japanese opinion molders,
amid the rush to smooth over the incident, were thinking about
the longer-term implications of the U.S. action. Japanese business
leaders, notes Kimihiro Masamura, an economist at Tokyo's Sen-
shu University, "are not aware of the extent of the impact they
have had on their foreign competitors over the past several years.
Now the Japanese have no other choice but to think globally."

However, for many other, more ordinary Japanese, the U.S.
sanctions were both a puzzlement and a frustration. Says Kenji
Hatakenaka, 38, a project-development manager at Sharp electronics: "It's hard for me to see what's really behind this. Japan
doesn't pose the kind of threat you would expect to provoke such
a reaction." Hatakenaka claims that the Nakasone government's
efforts to boost consumption in response to U.S. pressure are
running into resistance at the rice-roots level. Says he: "The gov-

ernment tells us to spend, but with currency instability everyone feels it's safer to save. The government says, 'Buy that TV today,' but we'd rather wait until the price comes down."

In some cases, Japanese dismay at the sanctions is also taking an unpleasant turn. Surveys by Prime Minister Nakasone's office show a conspicuous decline in Japanese affections for the U.S. The most recent sounding in October revealed that 67.5% of the sampling felt themselves to be friendly toward the U.S., down from 75.6%. The October reading was the lowest pro-American result since the prime ministerial surveys were started in 1978.

For Nakasone, a more important question is how many Japanese are still friendly toward him. The answer may be not many. The Prime Minister will know better after nationwide local elections on April 12, when he and the ruling Liberal Democratic Party are now expected to take a drubbing. The main reason for that is not the U.S. trade dispute but Nakasone's announced decision to impose an unpopular 5% national sales tax. Nakasone has not made a single appearance on behalf of local candidates— because no invitations were extended to him. Jokes one Tokyo academic: "If President Reagan is a lame duck, our Prime Minister is a dying duck." Nakasone probably did not feel any better after U.S. Trade Representative Yeuter told a Senate Finance Committee hearing that he could not understand why Japan was planning to introduce the value-added tax. Replied Japanese Government Spokesman Masaharu Gotoda: "The tax system is our country's internal affair."

U.S.-Japanese trade difficulties, not to mention relations between the two countries in general, may become slightly frostier after the Prime Minister leaves the scene. Observes Larry Niksch, an Asian affairs specialist at the Congressional Research Service: "Nakasone and Reagan have been the glue that has kept the relation close. Below them there is a good deal of animosity on both sides. That could cause serious damage later."

The harsh fact is that the effort to manage relations between the close friends and allies cannot improve while the U.S. trade balance remains so badly out of kilter. This year many economists foresee no more than a $30 billion improvement in the trade deficit, and quite a few see less. Even worse, the U.S. trade balance will have to improve more than the current deficit indicates because the country is now an international debtor. In the current issue of the quarterly *Foreign Affairs*, Harvard Economist Martin

Feldstein, a former chairman of President Reagan's Council of Economic Advisers, estimates that during the 1990s the U.S. will need to generate $60 billion annually just to repay the interest and principle on its burgeoning foreign debt. According to Washington Economist Bergsten, the pressure will thus be on to create a $200 billion improvement in the American trade balance. That is liable to add to the considerable trade ferment on Capitol Hill. As Senate Majority Leader Robert Byrd puts it, "It is time to make more pragmatic use of our leverage."

That pressure will be borne not just by Japan but by all of America's trading partners. Fear of U.S. protectionism is a considerable motivation, for example, behind Canada's desire to conclude a historic free-trade agreement with Washington that would remove tariffs and most other trade barriers between the two countries during the next 15 years or so. President Reagan was to endorse that effort once again in a meeting with Canadian Prime Minister Brian Mulroney on a one-day state visit to Ottawa this week. But other close U.S. allies fear they may eventually be left out in the cold. Says a top European Community trade official in Brussels: "What worries us is that the U.S.-Japanese trade deficit will be balanced on the backs of the Europeans."

Avoiding that kind of protectionist debacle will take considerable American self-discipline. Among other things, policymakers must speedily reduce the federal budget deficit, which has fueled so much excess U.S. consumption. But there will also have to be considerable changes in U.S. corporate and educational culture. American businessmen, who have traditionally paid most of their attention to domestic markets, must become more aggressive in going after foreign sales. American managers also need to take a leaf out of Japanese manuals about greater worker involvement in product quality control. The U.S. education system needs vast improvement before it can produce blue-collar graduates on a par with Japanese production workers. If U.S. businessmen want to penetrate foreign markets, there will have to be much greater emphasis in U.S. schools on the successful learning of foreign languages.

More, rather than less, openness in both the U.S. and Japan would also help. Japan's need to reinvest its surplus cash is one impetus driving the country ever closer to the U.S. Another is Washington's need for Japanese funds to finance the budget deficit. Notes Goldman Sachs' Hormats: "Japan and the U.S. are locked in an embrace from which there is no escape. It may create some discomfort, but there is no longer any way out of it."

The question remains of how much discomfort—not to mention occasional pain—may be involved. If, as the Reagan Administration hopes, the semiconductor skirmish spurs Tokyo to more urgent efforts to settle trade disputes, it will have served a useful purpose.

The history of trade sanctions, however, shows how dangerous commercial conflicts can be. One sobering example dates back to 1941, when the U.S. and other Western powers imposed sanctions on the export of iron and manganese to Japan for its incursions into Manchuria. That embargo played a role in the Japanese decision to attack Pearl Harbor. Nothing remotely similar in the way of hostility, of course, looms in the current trade battle. But as the two sides confront each other, they need to be acutely aware that deep antagonisms over trade can often contain the seed of future disaster.

JAPAN MAKES THE HIT LIST[5]

George Bush sat in the Oval Office last Thursday morning, fretting once again about Japan. For months he and his aides had debated one of the most delicate issues they have faced: whether to put Japan on a "hit list" of countries charged with unfair trading practices. Just three days earlier, some of his advisers, at least, thought Bush had put the matter to rest. Despite enormous pressure from Congress and his own Commerce Department, the president seemed to be leaning against naming Japan as a "priority" violator under the so-called Super 301 law—a designation that could lead to general trade retaliation after 18 months. As one Commerce Department staffer in favor of getting tougher with Tokyo put it: "We thought we had been rolled."

Commerce did seem to have lost the battle—until trade hawks in Congress got word that Bush might be backing down.

[5]Reprint of an article by Bill Powell, *Newsweek* staffwriter. Reprinted by permission from *Newsweek*, June 5, 1989. Copyright © 1989, Newsweek, Inc. All rights reserved.

White House staffers started getting angry calls from Democrats and Republicans alike. Bush himself spoke with Democratic Sen. Don Riegle of Michigan and Republican Sen. John Danforth of Missouri. They delivered the same message: Congress had passed the new trade law requiring designation of "priority countries"—not just egregious individual trade practices. And Congress had Japan in mind. After all, it's Japan that accounts for more than a third of America's trade deficit—$55 billion out of last year's $138 billion total. Despite concessions from Tokyo, official and hidden trade barriers continue to play a role in sustaining that surplus.

Swayed by the 11th-hour lobbying, Bush picked up the big stick—then moved to soften the blow. To make sure Japan wasn't the only country getting a public flogging, he also cited India and Brazil as international trade villains. As for specific grievances, he decided the United States would consider retaliation for Japan's alleged failure to buy three types of U.S. products: supercomputers, satellites and processed lumber. (In a preliminary Commerce report issued in April, Japan was associated with alleged trading violations in 30 areas.) United States Trade Representative Carla Hills will lead negotiations about the three issues. But to resolve broader differences, Bush also set up a special negotiating committee, chaired by Secretary of State James Baker and Treasury Secretary Nicholas Brady. Their group is to commence trade talks with Tokyo that are free of legally mandated retaliatory threats.

The compromise appeared to placate Congress for the moment. "This is a very important symbolic step," said Sen. Max Baucus, Democrat of Montana. "The U.S. government has finally, officially acknowledged that Japanese trade practices are a significant trade problem." State Department officials gently suggested to Japanese counterparts that it was in Japan's interest to make concessions to Congress. Had Japan been left off the list, congressmen might have demanded an even tougher trade law. The Super 301 provisions under which Bush acted required the president to designate priority countries and practices by May 30; if the cited countries don't remove their alleged trade impediments within 12 to 18 months, Bush is required to retaliate by reducing their exports to the United States through tariffs or quotas.

The announcement last week ended a brutal behind-the scenes fight within the administration. On one side was a get-tough lobby led by Secretary of Commerce Robert Mosbacher, and Trade Representative Hills. On the other was a "free trade" school that included Richard Darman, director of the Office of Management and Budget, and Michael Boskin, chairman of the Council of Economic Advisers. Darman and Boskin argued that retaliation against U.S. trading partners could erode the foundations of the postwar economic order and eventually ignite a trade war. Mosbacher and Hills reflected a growing sentiment that some countries only pay lip service to free trade—and will open their markets only under stronger U.S. pressure.

The two sides staked out their positions early on. Hills came into office last January saying she would wield a "crowbar" to pry open foreign markets. Mosbacher openly lectured Japan and other nations, saying they had to buy more products from the United States or risk retaliation. Fellow members of the administration immediately labeled him a "protectionist." Boskin went public with those sentiments three weeks ago. Like most mainstream economists, he believes tariffs and quotas drive up prices on traded goods, contribute to inflation and, ultimately, lower real incomes. Trade-inhibiting tariffs were a major cause of the Great Depression of the 1930s, and that's the scenario Boskin conjured up: "If we wind up with a series of these retaliatory measures with our trade partners . . . It will not only cause a recession in the United States, it will cause a worldwide recession."

Some State Department officials privately pressed Bush to go easy on Japan for political reasons. They argued that Tokyo could not respond effectively to U.S. pressure. After a month of searching, no successor had been found for Prime Minister Noboru Takeshita, who has announced plans to resign after being linked to a widening stock-for-influence scandal. The leading candidates at the weekend were Foreign Minister Sousuke Uno and former prime minister Takeo Fukuda. In his confirmation hearings, Michael Armacost, the new U.S. ambassador to Japan, said he wants to be "the first commercial officer of the embassy." But embassy cables sent out under Armacost's name warned that blasting Japan as a trade villain would prompt "an emotional outburst" in Tokyo.

A showdown in the White House early last week seemed to persuade Bush to back off. Boskin, Darman and State Depart-

ment counselor Robert Zoellick argued that citing Japan for protectionist trade policies would be hypocritical. Boskin ticked off
a list of U.S. industries that benefit from import restrictions:
steel, autos, machine tools, television, textile. He reminded Bush
he had run as a free-trader. Even Hills conceded that U.S. quotas
on sugar imports are a "disgrace." Maybe, joked Bush, "we ought
to take action against a whole bunch of countries—including
ourselves."

Congress didn't buy the idea that the United States is just as
guilty as anyone of protecting its home market—and not without
reason. The United States may indulge in some protectionism,
but nowhere near as much as a number of its leading Asian and
European trading partners. In all, America has swept up $1.8 tril-
lion worth of foreign products over the last five years. When
congressional leaders started protesting, Bush relented.

It will be months before the consequences of putting Japan
on the hit list become clear. Ambassador Armacost, among others, has pointed out that "there's nothing wrong with being hard-
headed. The Japanese respect it." Japan publicly condemned the
action. Foreign Minister Uno called the 301 listing "extremely
regrettable." The United States, he said, was trying to "divert attention from the major cause of the trade imbalance": its own
macroeconomic policies. Japanese officials privately conceded
they knew 301 was coming, however, and Uno himself called for
continued "cooperation." For now that's what both seem to have
in mind. And for all the recent bluster, serious negotiation is still
the best way of avoiding a nasty trade war neither side wants.

IV. THE TRADE WAR CONTROVERSY

EDITOR'S INTRODUCTION

The controversy over fair-trade practices introduced in the previous section is elaborated upon more fully in Section Four. In the first article in this section, Bill Powell in *Newsweek* points out a number of the fallacies or myths involved in the dispute. The U.S. trade deficit, Powell asserts, is not necessarily a sign of economic weakness; indeed, the U.S. Gross National Product is greater now than when we ran a trade surplus in 1982. Nor is it true that the Japanese don't buy American products: the average Japanese citizen spends 1.7 percent of his total income on American goods, while Americans spend on a bit more, 1.8, on Japanese goods. Nor is it advisable that American manufacturers should be protected by import quotas or tariffs, since competition is precisely what compels U.S. companies to improve. In a following article written from a different perspective, John W. Dower in *The Nation* argues that the Japanese seem to non-Japanese to unfairly protect their home markets and to have an intransigent sense of cultural and ethnic superiority amounting to arrogance, thus arousing increasing frustration and anger.

However, in a speech delivered in 1989, U.S. Representative Richard A. Gephardt points out that systemic differences between the Japanese and the American economic models have obsoleted the standard meaning of terms like "tariff," "quota," and "free trade." Gephardt means that traditional remedies for problems like the ballooning U.S. trade deficit work no longer in a changing global marketplace—that, for example, shrinking the dollar may do little but accommodate the inevitable shrinkage of U.S. political power. In an article reprinted from *New Perspectives Quarterly*, David Halberstam, the author of *The Reckoning*, a study of how Detroit stumbled in its competition with Japanese auto makers, compares the humbling of the American military in Vietnam to the economic comeuppance of U.S. corporations at the hands of Japanese businesses. According to Halberstam, it was American arrogance that blinded policymakers to the unyielding nationalism of the Viet Cong and corporate arrogance that was blindsided by the Japanese economic miracle, which is yet another manifestation of Asian nationalism.

In an address reprinted from *Vital Speeches of the Day*, the journalist Seiichi Kamise urges restraint in "Japan-bashing," for some American businessmen simply refuse to learn about Japanese culture and customs, and points out that a Japanese-American divorce is politically, economically, and militarily impossible. In two following articles, by Professor Lawrence W. Beer from *Vital Speeches of the Day* and by diplomat William Clark, Jr. from the *Department of State Bulletin*, a history of the U.S.-Japanese alliance since the Second World War is sketched and arguments are advanced that the partnership will continue to serve the full range of political, economic, military, and cultural interests of both countries.

Another article, by Robert Neff and Paul Magnusson in *Business Week*, discusses the revisionist trend in American policy thinking of the late 1980s. The new revisionism, they point out, questions the former belief that Japan will eventually evolve into a more open economy and posits that pressures must therefore be brought to bear that will move Japan into a more equitable market arrangement. In a following article, George R. Packard in *Foreign Affairs* reviews the background of the Japanese-U.S. dispute, and concludes that Japan cannot continue to protect its home market while running large exporting surpluses year after year. What is needed particularly, Packard believes, is an independent bilateral agency, a "Wisemen's Commission," to formulate a "Japan policy" that would mediate trade differences and achieve equity before animosity on both sides becomes explosive. In a final article, also in *Foreign Affairs*, Mike Mansfield pleads for a cooling of tempers and mutual recognition of the benefits of the U.S.-Japanese partnership, "the most important relationship in the world, bar none."

THE MYTHS OF A TRADE WAR[1]

They don't make stock-market crashes—or trade wars—like they used to. It was all there, every piece of a frightening puzzle: rapidly falling stock prices, a weakening currency, an onerous tariff slapped on a major trading partner and, most ominously, talk of a wider trade war. Gloomy headlines and doomsday scenarios abounded. March 30, 1987—Black Monday.

The panic lasted one day. Black Monday suddenly transformed itself into a buying opportunity of monumental proportions. After plunging 80 points in the first hour on Monday, the market recovered a bit and finished down 57 for the day. Then, in the bionic bull's most remarkable show of strength to date, the market continued to rise, muscling up a stunning 70 points on Friday to close up 54 for the week. There was a surreal quality to the rise, coming so closely after rumors of economic war. Some economists remain convinced the market is in a dangerous, speculative phase and that Monday was merely a warning.

Could they be right? Perhaps. If the doomsday nightmares become real, it will likely be because history repeats itself on one key issue: trade. Few economic issues are more complex, and few issues have become more politicized, than trade. The financial markets' performance last Monday demonstrated how dangerous that combination can be. "What the market was reminding the politicians on Monday was simple," says economist Alan Reynolds. "The Smoot-Hawley tariff caused the Great Depression. That was the message." But the market's violent reaction to protectionist winds set the stage for the rebound: it led investors to believe they had put the fear of God into the politicians. "On Tuesday people came to feel things weren't as bad as they had thought they were on Monday," says Robert Hormats, a former Carter administration official now at Goldman Sachs; "there was a feeling things weren't breaking down."

That feeling may have to be reinforced time and again to avert disaster. The politicization of trade has led to the creation of an array of myths, half-truths and outright falsehoods about

[1]Reprint of an article by Bill Powell, *Newsweek* staffwriter. Reprinted by permission from *Newsweek*, April 13, 1987. Copyright © 1987 Newsweek, Inc. All rights reserved.

how the world trading system works. Politicians, economists and journalists peddle them blithely—and they are rarely countered. The myths about trade have become so ingrained that the debate in Washington seems to have shifted fundamentally: the question now isn't whether to engage in a trade war, but rather which weapons will be carried into battle and how lethal they should be. Yet much of what policymakers assume these days is at best debatable—and arguably just plain wrong. Here are four whoppers:

• *The trade deficit is a sign of economic weakness.* When the U.S. dollar soared in value against other currencies between 1982 and 1984, many U.S. goods were priced out of world markets. The country's trade deficit soared. Now, with the dollar down 45 percent against the Japanese yen, the trade deficit hangs stubbornly high—$170 billion or so. Conclusion? The United States is an economic basket case, hurtling down the same road traveled by Britain, once an economic power, now an industrial cripple. And compared with Japan, with whom we have a $58 billion trade deficit, America already seems second rate.

In fact, the trade deficit may not signify anything that anyone needs to lose sleep over. C. Fred Bergsten, an assistant secretary of the treasury in the Carter administration, writes that "bilateral balances in themselves are neither a meaningful indicator of international competitiveness nor a sensible guide for policy." Herbert Stein, chairman of the Council of Economic Advisers under President Nixon, goes Bergsten one better. He believes the government can simply ignore the trade deficit. "It will end when Americans are no longer willing to borrow enough or foreigners are no longer willing to lend enough to finance it. These borrowers and lenders have a lot of their own money at stake and are at least as well informed and as well motivated as the government to decide when the deficit has gone too far." This is the classic free-market view, and critics counter that adhering to it means ceding economic superiority to Japan in order to remain ideologically pure.

But consider: in the United States gross national product and output per person are both higher now than when the country last ran a trade surplus (1982). And it's not just hamburgers and junk bonds the United States produces: from November 1982 to November 1986 American manufacturing output increased 30 percent, outpacing any other major industrialized country. Including Japan.

• *The Japanese don't buy American.* It's true, the average Japanese citizen spends slightly less of his total income on American goods than Americans do for Japanese goods. But it's close: 1.7 percent to 1.8 percent. Why then is the trade imbalance between the two countries so pronounced? Mainly because the U.S. companies that have successfully penetrated the Japanese market have done so from within—not by exporting goods into the country. Says Roger Johnson, chairman of Western Digital Corp., a semiconductor producer with operations in Japan: "You have trouble doing business there unless you are doing business *right* there. To crack that market you damn well better understand the uniqueness or you'll fail." Many other companies agree. A recent study by Enzio von Pfeil, an economist with the London-based brokerage house Smith New Court, shows that sales of U.S. subsidiaries operating in Japan are four times larger than the U.S. trade deficit with Japan. He says Japan would import 174 percent more goods from the United States if it weren't for the Japanese operations of U.S. companies.

Some American subsidiaries in Japan export products to the United States. Texas Instruments, for example, runs a highly efficient chip plant in Japan and sends a portion of the products home. Such shipments get counted in the trade statistics as a Japanese import in the United States. Kenichi Ohmae, a managing director at McKinsey & Co., argues that trade statistics as currently reported distort economic reality. "They're practically irrelevant," he says.

• *The Japanese unfairly protect their markets. If they opened them up the trade issue would go away.* The Japanese *do* shield some key domestic industries with standard protectionist barriers. They have also erected so-called nontariff barriers that make life complicated and frustrating for many foreign companies. These include ridiculously detailed specifications that frequently must be met before products will be allowed in the country. Still, Ohmae believes if the Japanese removed all such trade barriers, America's $58 billion trade deficit with Japan would fall by only $12 billion. Mike Mansfield, the U.S. ambassador to Japan, estimates $15 billion. That still leaves the United States with a worldwide trade deficit of $155 billion. The reason, in part, is that the United States and Japan do not operate their economies in a vacuum. In some cases the United States would not step in and be the low-cost supplier. "Take meat," a protected industry in Japan, says

Ohmae. Australia and Argentina would both undercut the United States. A corollary to this myth is that *if* the Japanese opened up they would be hurt economically. Not so, argues Richard Blackhurst, chief economist to the General Agreement on Tariffs and Trade. Japanese consumers would pay lower prices because their industries would face more competition.

• *Japan is an economic juggernaut. The U.S. government needs to help its companies become more competitive if they are to survive.* The Japanese have serious problems: the rising yen hurts and growth has all but stopped. They have an aging work force, a younger generation that may not be as hardworking as their parents and they face stiff competition from the so-called Asian tigers—South Korea, Taiwan, Singapore. These countries, with their low-priced labor, have targeted basic industrial markets (autos and consumer electronics) with a vengeance. In other words, they are doing to Japan what Japan did to the United States.

Some U.S. companies still aren't as efficient as Japan's best today. But more are getting there, precisely because they felt competition's lash. Robert Neely, a consultant to the semiconductor industry for McKinsey, believes the penalties on Japanese chips will actually hurt American industry in the long run. "It takes away the pain, and no pain—no gain." By no means are all U.S. companies getting whipped internationally: since 1980, 100 companies in a group called the American Business Conference have increased sales overseas 27 percent annually. Many of them, says ABC's chairman, Arthur Levitt Jr., identify niche markets and capitalize on technological advances—reinforcing the notion that individual firms themselves, and not the government, will determine whether the United States is "competitive."

Protectionism may be the swine-flu vaccine of the 1980s: the cure for which there is no known disease. Some policymakers hold out hope that this year, despite the current rhetoric in Washington, Congress will not enact tough trade legislation. Says Hormats: "They want to be seen as tough, but not protectionist." That's a difficult trick. In the past, Congress has usually backed off from egregious legislation—after snarling angrily for the folks back home. The final myth—that Congress wants to get tough on trade—may now be turning into reality.

THE END OF INNOCENCE[2]

In 1979 Harvard University sociologist Ezra Vogel published a book that provoked mild interest in the United States but became a sensational best seller in Japan. The book, *Japan As Number One*, describes in a very positive manner the ingredients of the Japanese "miracle."

At that time, the trade imbalance between Japan and the United States was a few billion dollars, and Japan's total foreign investments were negligible. Today, despite the recent appreciation of the yen, Japan's trade surplus with the United States is in the neighborhood of $60 billion, its worldwide trade surplus is almost $90 billion, its net international assets (investment abroad minus debt owed to foreigners) are estimated to be near $200 billion and Professor Vogel's catchy phrase has become commonplace on both sides of the Pacific.

Commonplace also is the understanding of what "Japan As Number One" really means. It means "America As Number Two": the end of the postwar economic supremacy of the United States, the end of a global capitalist system dominated by the white powers, the ascendance of the Pacific over the Atlantic as the hub of world commerce.

To Americans, this is shocking. To the Japanese, it is exhilarating. And to virtually everyone, including a great variety of knowledgeable Japanese, the sudden confluence of Japan's ascendancy and America's decline is awkward, ominous and potentially explosive.

Cynics may observe a certain ironic continuity in the current situation: Now, as in the past, the "Pacific partners" appear to be incapable of sustaining a genuinely equitable relationship. Under the bilateral alliance that emerged out of the postwar occupation of Japan, for decades it was accepted without question by both sides that Japan would operate in America's shadow. In the parlance of the Japanese left, this was "dependent independence" or "subordinate independence" within the postwar Pax Americana.

[2]Reprint of an article by John W. Dower, professor of history and Japanese studies at the University of California, San Diego. Reprinted by permission from *The Nation*, September 12, 1987. Copyright © 1987 by The Nation Company, Inc.

Now the tables are turned. The relationship is still unequal, but suddenly it is the United States that finds itself economically (but not militarily) dependent. Neither side has yet shown itself capable of working out a relationship that involves genuine equality and reciprocity.

That is ominous indeed. Among close observers of the U.S.-Japan relationship, there is virtually no one who believes the current imbalance can continue without catastrophic consequences, not only to the two countries but to the world economy. The two sides simply must bring their economies into closer balance. Yet at the same time, it is difficult to find among those same commentators anyone who is sanguine about whether the crisis can be resolved. Doomsday scenarios are everywhere and come in an almost infinite variety of guises. Broadly speaking, however, it is possible to discern four general strains in the American response to Japan's emergence as an economic juggernaut:

• Genuine admiration of the so-called Japanese miracle.

• Growing skepticism, at least in some circles, concerning Japan's ability to keep producing miracles in the face of impending social and economic challenges.

• Heightened emphasis on the peculiar nature of Japanese capitalism, which not only undermines the once-cherished dream of Japan as a capitalist model for industrializing countries but also makes it impossible to be optimistic about Japan's ability to "internationalize" its domestic economy in any serious way.

• Mounting resentment at what is widely perceived to be narrow economic nationalism and even racial arrogance among many Japanese.

In the final analysis, resolution of the current U.S.-Japan economic crisis will depend on a deep reservoir of good will and not just technocratic savvy. Thus, the continued existence of positive American attitudes toward Japan deserves emphasis. While Japan-bashing has become a popular pastime in many sectors of U.S. society, it is still virtually impossible to go anywhere in the country today without encountering admiration for the work habits and economic accomplishments of the Japanese. For every auto worker in Detroit who participates in the symbolism of smashing a Toyota, there are countless other workers who admire—and purchase—Japanese products. And for every Lee Iacocca–type capitalist who blames U.S. competitive failures on Japan's refusal to "play on a level field," numerous other corporate heads are sending their executives to sessions on Japanese-style management.

In Japan too, where recent opinion polls show a decline in respect for American capabilities and accomplishments, it is important to note that the cup is also half full. Despite such negative trends, friendly feelings toward Americans and American life styles remain high throughout Japanese society. There is also, however, a new school of thought in the United States that focuses on the vulnerability of the Japanese economy and the grave problems that loom ahead for that country. In seizing on this theme, Western commentators are actually echoing a gloomy prognostication popular in many Japanese circles.

Much of the fascination of this line of analysis lies in its double edge: On the one hand, it is suggested that the current crisis in trade and capital-flow imbalances has been exaggerated, that the Japanese bubble will burst or at least be deflated in the near future. On the other hand, such preoccupation with Japan's vulnerability contributes to the general impression of a worldwide crisis in capitalism by suggesting that—like the debt-ridden Third World and United States—even Japan's great creditor economy is imperiled.

Representative of this line of thought was a lengthy and comprehensive special report titled "Japan's Troubled Future" in the March 30 issue of *Fortune*. Among the impending troubles *Fortune* called attention to were: the rapidly increasing number of senior citizens in Japan; the probable decline of lifetime employment; the continued inability of Japanese schools to stimulate genuinely creative thinking, especially at the university level, because of the traditional emphasis on rote learning; the greater preoccupation of young Japanese with personal and family affairs; an aging industrial plant; declining industries, particularly coal, steel, shipbuilding and consumer electronics; an acute housing shortage; mounting foreign pressures to open the domestic economy to international competition and investment; and rising suspicion abroad about Japan's willingness to engage in genuine cooperation with other nations and peoples.

Citing a similar list of Japanese weaknesses, *Newsweek*'s coverage of the trade crisis last spring concluded that "the Japanese have serious problems." *Newsweek* also called attention to the threat to Japan (and the United States and Europe as well) from what is sometimes called Asia's "gang of four": South Korea, Taiwan, Hong Kong and Singapore.

Even Japanese management practices, which have enjoyed remarkable romanticization and praise in the West over the past five or ten years, are beginning to come under fire. Nissan Motors, for example, recently indicated that it might file a lawsuit against *The Progressive* for an article the magazine ran about employee grievances in the company's much-ballyhooed plant in Smyrna, Tennessee. The prediction of the Keidanren, Japan's most powerful federation of corporate leaders, that the majority of Japanese business ventures in the United States will fail has been widely quoted in the U.S. media.

On the American side, there is a hint of grim solace in some of those commentaries. Being number one did not last long for us, the implication seems to be, and it will last even less long for Japan.

Recently, however, another line of equally pessimistic analysis has begun to emerge. While capitalists outside Japan continue to give close attention to the viability of the so-called Japanese model, it is becoming increasingly fashionable in academic as well as political circles to argue that Japan's economic structure has in fact been shaped by cultural and historical forces in ways that make it fundamentally unique. That argument was forcefully made in the summer issue of the *Journal of Japanese Studies*, the major U.S. journal devoted entirely to Japan. In what is an unusual special issue on the "trade crisis," some of the West's leading Japan specialists offer powerful ammunition to those who argue that—for institutional as well as political and psychological reasons—the Japanese will find it difficult if not impossible to restructure their domestic economy in ways that seriously contribute to rectifying trade and investment imbalances.

The structural barriers to internationalizing the domestic Japanese economy (or web of government and company relationships) are so great as to be almost insurmountable, the argument goes. Furthermore, expanding domestic consumption would entail abandoning the very practices that facilitated rapid economic growth in the first place (long work hours, untaxed savings, preferential policies for producers and exporters, etc.), and psychological resistance to that would be enormous. Finally, the rather tight controls by which conservative leaders once guided Japan Inc. have come unbundled and been replaced by a multitude of contentious political and economic elements.

University of California, Berkeley, political scientist Chalmers Johnson, an authority on Japan's industrial policy, argues that not only has Japan "invented and put together the institutions of capitalism in new ways, ways that neither Adam Smith nor Karl Marx would recognize or understand," but in the process it has created "not a success story but a supply-side monster." Johnson also notes that the much-publicized Maekawa report of April 1986, issued by a blue-ribbon commission of private citizens appointed by Prime Minister Yasuhiro Nakasone, acknowledged how skewed Japan's industrial policy has been and called for drastic reform. Should such reform not be forthcoming, he concludes, Japan "will soon find itself ostracized by the rest of the world."

How the "monster" can be expected to change its very nature Johnson does not clearly indicate. And, in fact, the Maekawa report met a hostile reception in Japan. It was criticized for, among other things, not recognizing that the real responsibility for the current crisis lies not with Japan but with the United States. Many Japanese maintain that Americans are simply making scapegoats of the Japanese for problems of their own making. The Americans, the counterargument goes, lack the discipline and resolve to tighten their belts, pay their debts, restructure their economy and restore U.S. competitiveness.

Implicit in such Japanese criticism of U.S. economic practices, of course, is pride in the distinctive features of Japanese capitalism. And in its more extreme forms, such pride has begun to feed a rising tide of neonationalism and outright racial arrogance. Resentment toward such attitudes constitutes the fourth conspicuous strain in current U.S. criticism of Japan.

In part, as many Americans admit, Japanese expressions of national and racial pride represent a kind of sweet revenge for the numerous slights the Japanese had to endure during the decades of "subordinate independence." It is understandable that people who were publicly described by General Douglas MacArthur as being like 12-year-old children and privately demeaned as "little Sony salesmen" and "small and petty bookkeepers" (reportedly by Henry Kissinger) should take special pleasure in reversing roles and addressing Americans and Europeans as parent to child, teacher to pupil, creditor to debtor. Increasingly, however, legitimate pride in the nation's achievements has given way to expressions of outright arrogance.

"The arrogance of power" is of course a phrase that became associated with the United States in the heyday of its postwar expansion. There is, however, an intriguing difference in the Japanese case: American arrogance tends to have an extroverted quality, expressed in the notion that it is both possible and desirable to export the American way to the rest of the world. By contrast, the new Japanese arrogance points inward, an opposite direction. Although there is still much talk about the Japanese model, there is even more talk by Japanese these days about the "uniqueness," "homogeneity" and "purity" of Japanese society.

The basic message non-Japanese now seem to be hearing from Japan is, The reason we are number one is that we Japanese are biologically and culturally unique in ways no one else can ever emulate.

That was the real thrust of Prime Minister Nakasone's notorious comments a year ago about the negative impact of ethnic minorities in the United States. In expressing his contempt for nonwhites in America, he was implicitly saying what is often said outright in Japan nowadays: that Japan is a superior nation because it is monoracial. Nakasone is actually a fascinating example of the complexity of those trends, for he is simultaneously a genuine supporter of the intellectual as well as economic internationalization of Japan and a fervent nationalist who officially venerates the war dead of World War II, believes in the special destiny of Nippon (a jingoistic way of reading the ideograms for Japan, usually pronounced "Nihon") and clearly believes in the superiority of *Yamato damashii* ("Japanese spirit," a potent slogan during World War II).

While the Japanese media are diligent in reporting examples of slurs by foreigners, most Japanese seem unaware of how carefully their own ethnocentric expressions are being monitored abroad. A recent American review of Akio Morita's autobiography, *Made in Japan*, for example, called attention to his references to "our one-race nation," as well as what the Sony chair called "a kind of Oriental sixth sense." In his book *Japan's Modern Myth*, linguist Roy Andrew Miller has described the persistent ridicule of *hen na gaijin* ("queer foreigners") on Japanese television. James Fallows, reporting from Japan for *The Atlantic* just before Nakasone's gaffe about American minorities, dwelled at great and bitter length on the pervasive sense of racial exclusion that all Westerners in Japan are made to feel. Ian Buruma, arts and society editor of the *Far Eastern Economic Review*, recently wrote several widely discussed articles about Japan's neonationalist *Minzoku-ha* intellectuals and politicians, whom he likened to the Volkists in Nazi Germany. In Japan itself, one of the most vigorous growth industries of recent years is an ongoing debate known as the *Nihonjin-ron*, involving discussion at every conceivable level of communication about what being Japanese really means.

In that atmosphere, it is not surprising that a large number of Americans and other non-Japanese view the current economic crisis as more than just a predictable example of capitalist competition or plain economic nationalism on the part of Japan. In innumerable ways, they hear the Japanese themselves saying they are a unique race with a superior culture that is closed to outsiders. That the domestic Japanese market also seems impenetrable is consistent with that larger picture.

As any visitor to Japan quickly learns, *gaijin*, the Japanese word for "foreigner," is written with two characters that mean, literally, "outside person." And as the Japanese seem strangely slow to learn, the non-Japanese response to being kept an outsider—beyond the pale in so many ways—is frustration, resentment, anger and, increasingly, outbursts of rage.

Such a situation, in which seemingly intractable material problems have become so intertwined with national pride and visceral emotions, offers little room for optimism.

U.S.-JAPANESE TRADE RELATIONS:
GREAT NECESSITIES CALL OUT GREAT VIRTUE[3]

Recently, I heard a story about George Bush being in a coma for three years and waking to find Dan Quayle standing at his bedside. Upon seeing the Vice President, the President begins to ask a few questions.

After asking how long he has been asleep he inquires about the state of the U.S. economy. To his surprise, Quayle tells him that the budget and trade deficits have been reduced to zero.

[3]Reprint of a speech by Richard A. Gephardt, United States Representative from Missouri. *Vital Speeches of the Day*. My. 15, '89. Reprinted with permission.

Then, President Bush asks about inflation, which he figures must be at an all time high. Again, to his surprise, Quayle says that inflation is not a problem. Having his doubts, the President asks for specifics. "How much," he asks "does a first class stamp cost?" "Very reasonable," Quayle responds—"only 30 Yen."

Unfortunately, this anecdote contains a kernel of truth. When I look at America today, I see some of the real challenges confronting us. I see a slow decline of our competitive edge, a steady loss of control of our economic destiny, and a systematic inability on the part of both government and business to meet the challenges. I don't know if President Bush saw these challenges while he was in Tokyo and Seoul and Beijing—but I hope you do.

I want to talk to you this morning about why I think those problems are out there. I want to talk to you about the grave danger of losing control of our economic destiny—and the trade deficit, productivity problems, and domestic debt that are symptomatic of the problem.

But I didn't come here just to talk about problems—I came to talk about solutions. About one solution that's being tried, and isn't working. And three more solutions I want to try.

In 1970, our trade surplus was $800 million, and we had run trade surpluses for 24 years in a row—since the end of WWII. By 1988 our trade position had deteriorated so dangerously that talk of surpluses seemed like ancient history. Between 1970 and 1988, we accumulated a total trade deficit of more than $1 trillion, by running up deficits for 16 of those 18 years.

Right now the United States is the largest debtor nation in the history of the world. Our foreign debt now exceeds the debt of countries two through seven combined. That's right. If you added up the total debt of Brazil, Mexico, Argentina, Venezuela, the Philippines and Nigeria—you'd still have less total debt than the United States of America.

It's hard to pick up a financial paper today without reading an article exploring the wrenching question of how Mexico, Argentina and Brazil will ever cope with their debt. No one suggests they can ever run sufficient trade surpluses to even it out. That's assumed to be impossible, so it's only a matter of how they're going to pay it off—in *dollars*, of course.

But I haven't read *any* articles speculating on how America will pay back its debt. We don't talk about it because we silently assume, I suppose, that future surpluses will offset today's deficit.

Sometime soon we have to ask the question: What will we sell foreigners to run a half trillion dollar surplus in the next few years? Will it be cameras, autos, steel, textiles, tires, semiconductors, computers, VCRs, televisions? These don't seem to be likely candidates—our industries are troubled or out of business. So what will it be? We are spared the pain of facing the problem squarely now because our foreign creditors apparently also aren't thinking the unthinkable. They're financing our debt without so much as a murmur of dissent.

Like a one-rich pioneer family short on cash but long on pride, we are living off our reputation—our good name and little else. But the question is: How long will our reputation continue to carry us?

Three months ago I was in Japan, and I think I heard—far off in the distance—the faint rumblings of our reputation beginning to crack and crumble. It was not a pleasant sound.

At a meeting of Japanese business leaders, they suggested that since their investors were purchasing 30 percent of our treasury securities, we should consider denominating them in *Yen*—rather than *dollars*. They said such a move would be required to keep Japanese investors interested in purchasing U.S. securities.

It's like the local bank telling the members of that proud pioneer family that their credit is running out.

The unthinkable is becoming thinkable. Foreign investors are starting to question our ability to pay our debt. And as is always the case, the creditor is beginning to use his leverage on the debtor.

We wouldn't think of letting Argentina pay us in pesos because tomorrow or the next day the peso may be devalued again. Before long, Japan won't *ask* us to pay the debt in Yen—they will *tell* us. And we will comply. Our other creditors may soon follow with similar demands.

Creditors are strong. Debtors are weak. Creditors make demands. Debtors meet them. Creditors lead. Debtors follow. Creditors determine their destiny. Debtors don't.

Slowly, imperceptibly, we are losing control of our economic destiny. We are in danger of losing our greatest strength. Today's challenge is far different from those our country has already faced in this century—the First World War, the Great Depression, the outbreak of World War II, and the shock of Sputnik. In each of those the threat was sometimes slow in building but an immediate perceptible crisis finally erupted and pushed us into action.

Today the threat is much less visible: A year-by-year–week-by-week erosion of strength that comes from an inadequate education system, a stagnating standard of living and the steady downsizing of the American dream.

Some observers expect and predict we will eventually be faced with an urgent economic crisis that will push us into action. I believe these predictions are wrong. Much more likely is that because of the vacuum of leadership in the world and because our market for consumption remains so large other countries will prop up our false prosperity for a very long time.

Without a crisis, leaders must lead. No other issue will so seriously test the mettle of the Bush Presidency.

The appointment of James Baker—a man skilled in international finance—as Secretary of State stands in stark contrast to Ronald Reagan's choice of General Alexander Haig. I hope the choice signifies a long overdue recognition of the reality that it is our economic—and not our military—strength that is in danger around the globe.

President Bush's greatest mistake would be to rely simply on the Reagan trade policy. Its principal tenet was to attempt to overcome the trade deficit by devaluing the dollar, so American exports would be cheaper overseas, and foreign imports would be more expensive here. This was supposed to be a quick and painless cure to the problem. But this isn't just a *currency* problem. It's a leadership problem. Unfortunately, there's been all too little leadership on it.

In December, the trade deficit was up again to over $12 billion, which, when put into annual figures, comes to about $137 billion! At its worst, the trade deficit was $170 billion. A 50 percent devaluation of the dollar against the Yen and one third against the German Mark since its peak in February 1985, before the September 1985 Plaza Accord, only reduced the trade deficit by $25 billion. At this rate, what kind of devaluation would we need to remedy America's trade problem?

As I said, the problem was not caused only by the exchange rates, and twenty minutes into my recent trip to Japan I learned why the Reagan solution of devaluation, while some was needed, is no real solution at all. I hope the same lesson was learned by the four most important Americans at Hirohito's funeral—President Bush, and the three network anchors.

During my recent trip to Japan, our taxi ride from Narita Airport to our hotel in Tokyo was $170. Our hotel room was $350 a night. Our breakfast was $75. I doubt the President—or for that matter the anchors—were personally presented with such a tab. I hope they were, though, because they could learn more from one Tokyo restaurant check than from a dozen treatises on trade.

How many American businesses will now be able to afford to go to Japan to try to enter the market at those prices? Few or none.

If they looked, the President and the media also noticed something I saw on my last trip to Japan: the people seemed wealthier than they were when I went in 1982. One Japanese businessman made me understand why. He said: "Don't you understand why we're buying Honolulu and huge chunks of other American cities? You increased the wealth of Japan vis-à-vis the United States by 100 percent in one year—without us even lifting a *finger*."

I had never thought of it in those terms before. Because of the Reagan Administration's failed attempt at a quick fix, our greatest economic competitor now has a lot more wealth—a vital tool to create more productivity and wealth.

Finally, I confronted the ultimate folly of our devaluation scheme in a meeting with a number of Japanese writers and academics, where they discussed what they called "the second Japanese miracle." They said the first Japanese miracle was their recovery after World War II. The second miracle was their ability to accommodate a 100 percent appreciation of the Yen over the dollar without losing their market share in any area. The Japanese adjusted to the new currency rates quickly and their corporations made radical changes in manufacturing and work rules. The academics told how Japanese workers responded affirmatively to management demands for more productivity and less income.

Our remedy not only failed to weaken them—but far worse—it made our major competitor far stronger than before.

A look at recent productivity statistics tells the story. The productivity of the average Japanese worker increased by a total of 15.5 percent from 1982 to 1987. The American worker's productivity, on the other hand, has only increased 9.1 percent in those same 5 years. Relative to the U.S. worker's productivity level, Japanese worker's productivity capacity grew 6.4 percent during that period.

It is now apparent—painfully apparent—that devaluing the dollar was not enough. What is? I am proposing that we try three things: Change, change, and more change. Specifically, we must change the process of negotiating trade problems, change the practices of our trading partners, and change our own practices too.

First let's look at efforts to change the way the game is played—new ideas to change the way we negotiate out trade agreements.

First we must recognize that the important foreign trade barriers we face are no longer tariffs and quotas. Rather, what we often face today—especially in competition with industralized nations like Japan—are barriers that come from differences in our economic structures. For instance, we have anti-trust laws that are radically different than theirs, which produce corporate structures that are radically different than theirs. We must now question whether or how a level playing field can be constructed between us. Another example is distribution systems. Ours is wide open while Japan's is tightly controlled. Again, the mismatch between systems stifles "free trade."

For years we assumed we had created Japan in our own image after World War II and that it would respond to trade initiatives and rules as we do. Now we see that the problems there and with many other countries are much more complicated than that—and we must strive to execute a trade policy that attacks these real differences—and therefore barriers—and begin to change them.

Our present trade relations with many other countries are marked by a long series of specific disputes that cause overall mistrust and anger. Our present trade law calls for grievances to be lodged by individual American companies concerning alleged unfair trade practices against their products. Often we shy away from using tariffs and quotas as retaliation because such actions could hurt out own consumers, we fear counter retaliation, or we abhor using retaliatory acts. If the grievances by different companies in a particular industry are common and repetitive, negotiation with the offending country may begin, with the goal being a specific change in behavior to overcome the specific unfair practice.

There are several flaws with this procedure. First, we give all grievances equal status—no matter what their importance to the national interest. Some products, like semiconductors or computers, may be more important to maintaining our standard of living than others. The piecemeal approach is without priorities.

Second, the piecemeal approach produces so many separate, product-specific complaints that grievances against one nation may reach such a number as to create unbearable friction. That is about where we are today with a growing number of countries in East Asia and Europe.

Third, the procedure doesn't call for specific results or goals to be reached. We complain about widgets being excluded from a country's market—frustration with the slow grievance procedures leads to a long negotiation that leads to promises to do better. The procedure fails to produce results or ways to measure our trading partners' behavior.

Fourth, the process is weak on remedies or we are unusually reluctant to use them. Right now our trade negotiators are questioning if we should take retaliatory steps that we abhor and urge other countries to abhor. Our fear is that if we don't continue to reject retaliation we will lose our capacity to lead on these issues. I believe we must establish a new trade strategy and policy that contains the ability for necessary, albeit limited, retaliation to be used as a method of enforcement.

I believe the answer is as follows:

1. We must continue to achieve as much agreement on trade as we can in the multilateral setting—i.e. the Uruguay Round.

But we must realize that great progress is unlikely because the multilateral setting is not capable of resolving the multiplicity of complex nontariff issues that exist.

2. With highly industrialized competitors like East Asia and Europe, we must look to the practicality of bilateral—wholesale—agreements that solve as many complex disputes as possible at the same time. The U.S.-Canada Trade Treaty is one model that may show the way. However, this treaty is one that reflects the similarities of neighboring countries.

The next best candidate for such a bilateral agreement is Europe, especially as it moves toward 1992. Attempting this now with Japan may lead to nothing more than greater frustration. In East Asia and even Europe, the differences are greater and trade barriers more complex. Therefore, the negotiations will be all the more difficult.

3. Bilateral arrangements like the U.S.-Canada Treaty should include an arbitration panel to resolve disputes not covered by the treaty or that arise after its completion. It may be that an arbitration-like panel might be established between the U.S. and Japan in a limited area—before the negotiation of a bilateral treaty—to see if such an arrangement has promise and if ground rules can be established.

4. All such bilateral negotiations and agreements—whether general or by sector—should set out results or goals to be reached. The differences between market structures are often so great that failing to set goals ensures that no progress will be made. Sometimes the results called for will be market opening measures and at other times we will have to think in terms of percentage of market share because of the degree of difference in market structure.

5. We must use retaliatory remedies when appropriate. In the last few years the Reagan Administration finally took specific retaliatory actions when progress on a particular barrier was unobtainable in any other way. If such actions are taken judiciously and for good cause, they will not result in trade wars.

Our past reluctance to use retaliation has left us without a credible deterrent. The limited and judicious use of retaliation will keep our trading partners convinced that we mean business. Too many analysts have reacted to a raised voice at the bargaining table as if it were the last step before a trade war. If we adopted that same posture across the board we would have lost out to the Russians long ago.

Three additional matters that are not directly tied to the trade strategy issue must be mentioned.

First, because of the openness of our government, foreign countries find it easy to attempt to influence U.S. government trade and economic policy. But it's not nearly so easy for us to do the same in their countries.

For instance, it's hard to find a former U.S. trade negotiator who does not now represent foreign interests in Washington. It's estimated that the Japanese alone spend $100 million a year hiring Americans to influence U.S. policy. We would never be able to mount such an effort in Tokyo, even if we tried. The Japanese would cry out as we would if the Soviets started hiring former generals to lobby the Pentagon.

The Bush Administration must take steps to demand that Japan and other countries give us an equal chance to influence their economic policies. If they refuse, steps must be taken to overcome the inequality. If they won't let American businesses state their case for themselves, the American government must have the resolve to do it for them.

Second, we must ask for reciprocity regarding foreign investment. We want to invest in foreign countries, so we can hardly complain when they invest here. We must be willing to adopt reciprocal investment policies.

Third, we should be prepared to apply the new trade law allowing the President to prevent foreign takeovers of American firms where national security is possibly compromised. We cannot ignore concerns about selling off companies that may produce items crucial to our national security.

If all the steps I have described so far this morning were enacted tomorrow—if a sensible, centralized arbitration structure were established; if unfair trade barriers came tumbling down; and if the influence gap were closed immediately—we still would have achieved only half our goal. I was struck in my Presidential campaign by how difficult it is for all of us to think in two dimensions about our trade and competitiveness problems. Some want only to blame foreigners for our problems. Still others want only to blame us. We gravitate toward the mental laziness of thinking about the problem in only one dimension or the other.

The obvious truth is that there is fault on both sides and that our great challenge will not be met unless we can change other countries' behavior and *at the same time* change our own behavior. Where do we begin?

I do not have time today to cover it all. The challenges fall into two major categories. First, the government must create an economic environment in which private enterprises can prosper and grow. Second, the private sector must improve its performance at producing high quality products at a competitive price.

The governmental challenges are many—education, which is of paramount importance, research, and many others. But I would like to address only two today.

First, the Federal Government must lead by example. We must get our fiscal house in order so we have a proper environment for economic progress. This is not the time or the place for a protracted discussion of the federal budget mess, but suffice to say that without real cuts in agricultural subsidies and wasteful, duplicative weapons systems, as well as new revenue from an oil import fee, we will not even begin to dig out of the hole we're in. And although "kinder and gentler" in its hype, the Bush budget plan amounts to little more than rearranging the chairs on the deck of the fiscal Titanic left to us by the last Administration.

Next, we must reorganize—and streamline—the way the government deals with economic and trade issues. Right now, some 25 different agencies deal with trade in 25 different ways—but no one is looking at the big picture. We're like an affable sandlot football team going off to play the San Francisco 49'ers.

I am preparing legislation that will give us a coherent game plan. My proposals will gather most trade responsibilities into the Department of Commerce, create a National Economic Security Council, beef up the Foreign Commercial Service and better disseminate government research to the private sector.

"Perestroika" for our trade policy is a vital step. But if we don't have the people—seasoned, professional negotiators—to carry out that policy, all the reform in the world will be for naught.

An important but overlooked challenge facing the Bush Administration will be to convince our trade negotiators to make a career of it. The President's recent comments about the dignity of public service are an encouraging sign—and they're a welcome change after eight years of a gang that seemed to view government as a place to get your card stamped before you sell out and cash in.

An official of the Japanese Ministry of Trade and Industry recently asked me why we send "boys" to do a "man's" job at our trade negotiations. I think I know what he was driving at. Japan's top negotiators have been doing it for years and years. Our negotiators come and go in a few years—and more often than not wind up on foreign payrolls as lobbyists once we've trained them. The inexperience of our negotiators is a clear disadvantage in an arena in which history and experience are the primary tools of the trade.

In addition, perhaps because of our lack of organization on trade matters, our negotiators often lack a comprehensive agenda that outlines America's goals and priorities. We must send our negotiators into that room armed with a clear goal, and a sufficient supply of carrots and sticks to make that goal a reality.

Those are the changes I am trying to make in our government. But there are a host of changes you as business people must make as well. We have many well-run, productive corporations that can out-think, out-hustle and out-compete anyone anywhere in the world. The problem is, that group may be a minority in American business today. Perhaps Tom Peters has sold so many books on "excellence" in corporate America because it's such a rare find.

But don't take my word for it. Listen to some of the finest minds in American business today.

The business consultant, Robert Wood, warns that the U.S. in effect can't just ape the Japanese style of management. He said, and I quote, "We've got to recapture the enthusiasm, the pioneering spirit that made America a world leader."

H. Ross Perot, a pretty fair business person himself, says American managers are too often just "bean counters" today—passive, risk-averse, and lacking in leadership. He says our business schools fail to teach the most important leadership rule—the Golden Rule—that managers should treat employees the way they themselves would like to be treated.

All of this seems to revolve around attitudes, values and ethics. At one time American companies were known for their concern for excellence: for quality, for paying attention to the interests of their customers. At one time American corporate leaders traveled the globe, teaching the Japanese and the Europeans how to lead people and make products. At one time American corporations were known for their social and national responsibility. But now things have changed.

How far we have come from the day when American managers landed in Japan to help bring about the Japanese miracle—to today, when major American financiers have landed in jail for insider trading.

If George Bush does everything else right as President, yet fails to convince more of our corporate leaders that they must put excellence back into manufacturing and not just into financial manipulation—then he will ultimately fail as a President. For only the President has the "bully pulpit" to exert moral leadership on values.

It is my hope that our President will join in my efforts to fight for America's future. There is no intrinsic reason why this fight should be partisan—he's spoken of bipartisan cooperation, and this area badly needs it.

The hour is late and the time is short. The future is slipping away from us at an alarming rate. Each day a new layer of debt is added, another portion of our wealth is lost, and our position of economic weakness, and theirs of economic strength, is intensified and reinforced. Farmers, workers, young couples starting out already feel the loss of America's economic strength. They can't stand idly by as "business as usual" puts them out of business.

But judging from his Inaugural Address and his early actions, I fear our new President will not be willing to act boldly and decisively. He seems to be saying, "Don't worry, be happy." I am saying, "Don't sit there, do something."

The American people are equal to the challenge—let me assure you of that. All they need is the leadership that the people—and the times—demand.

Abigail Adams in 1780 captured perfectly the spirit of her time when she wrote to her husband: "These are times in which a genius would wish to live. It is not in the still calm of life, or in the repose of a pacific station, that great challenges are formed—great necessities call out great virtues."

I truly believe that—two hundred years after those words were written—America once again has entered a time in which a genius would wish to live. Two hundred years ago an untamed wilderness dotted with farms and a few scattered cities—a place we would today quite correctly call a Third World nation—faced the great challenges of its time and met them. The geniuses of those days built the strongest, freest, most dynamic nation in human history. And across two centuries and down ten generations it has been handed to us.

If I learned nothing else in 1987 and '88—as I traveled from Bettendorf, Iowa to Beaumont, Texas; from Concord, New Hampshire to Columbia, South Carolina; from Seattle, Washington to San Diego, California—I learned that the innate genius of the American people is still more than equal to the greatest challenge.

The question is whether you and I—the people entrusted with harnessing that genius and leading those people—will see the great necessities of our day, and call out the great virtues in the American people.

Thank you.

OF HUBRIS AND HONDAS[4]

In both *The Best and the Brightest*, a study of the policy-makers of the Vietnam War, and in *The Reckoning*, an account of competition between the Japanese and American auto industries, Pulitzer Prize–winning author David Halberstam documented how America's pride led to its fall.

In the following article, which first appeared in the Fall, 1987 issue of *NPQ*, Halberstam warns that we must discard the arrogance of success which has blinded this country to the abilities of nationalist guerrillas and economic competitors alike.

There are definite parallels between the American experience of confronting the Vietnamese in war and the Japanese in commercial competition. *The Best and the Brightest* is about the arrogance of power. *The Reckoning* is about the arrogance of affluence. Both books are about a nation that did not see the world was changing because it was caught up in its own myths.

World War II brought America kicking and screaming onto the scene of global power. We ended the war with more power than when we entered it. We were rich in a world that was poor. During the war we had pioneered in modern managerial systems and harnessed primitive computers to the industrial system. It seemed that the gods favored us and our power and affluence would go on forever. We perceived as a permanent condition that which was an historical fluke.

What happened in Vietnam and what is happening in America's industrial core today can be traced to the hubris caused by history's favor. We did not see the changing world. We did not give credit to other nations for being talented or for working hard. We squandered resources. Our business practices became astonishingly insular. One of my favorite quotes in *The Reckoning* is from former Michigan governor George Romney, talking about GM in the 1950s (and he might as well have been talking about America on the eve of entry into Vietnam): "Nothing is more vulnerable than entrenched success."

[4]Reprint of an article by David Halberstam, Pulitzer Prize–winning author. *New Perspectives Quarterly*. Fall '88. Reprinted with permission.

The McNamara Connection

The strategy of how to deal with Vietnamese nationalism was a product of the mentality of Ford Motor executives like Robert McNamara. He was the ultimate rational man who believed that the Viet Cong and North Vietnamese would act rationally, understand the power of technology, and end the war. During his time at Ford he was the symbol of the new modern business era, the new managerial class, with its numbers and computers, its contempt for tradition and the past, its contempt for the actual product, and for the old timers who knew how to make things.

The film *Platoon* brilliantly captures the fate of this mentality in the jungles of Vietnam. If you were a planner of that war, Vietnam looked like a small country and 500,000 men seemed like a lot of troops. But that steamy land swallowed up those US troops who, for all their might, could only control the ground on which they stood. *Platoon* shows how the terrain and the night deflect American technology, how power gets sucked down in a rice paddy. Soon the hunter becomes the hunted in this alien land and in this endless darkness. In the end of this movie, the commanders are calling in fire on their own men.

The Mistake of Disrespect

In Vietnam, we made the most serious mistake a power can make. We were not respectful of the enemy. By 1961, there was already considerable evidence that the enemy was very good. The Viet Cong were both tough and brave. They had a political system that provided endless recruits and they had brilliant leadership from top to bottom. They were an expression of powerful Asian nationalism and their system worked. We quite deliberately chose not to see that and defined the country's conflict in terms of communism and anti-communism.

Among Detroit auto executives, there was comparable contempt for the Japanese even as they were becoming an extraordinary new industrial player. In the mid 1970s when the Japanese built the best steel industry in the world, the joke among American automakers was, "If you scratch the door of a Japanese car, you can see the Budweiser can." That kind of foolish disrespect was right out of Vietnam.

When the Japanese first came here with autos in 1959, they made every mistake in the book. They brought small, underpowered, tank-like cars. But anyone who was paying attention could tell by 1966 they were getting very good.

They learned. They listened to the customers. They read American consumer magazines like bibles while Detroit executives thought they were edited by Ralph Nader. By 1968 Datsun brought out the 510, a very good car. Auto enthusiasts loved it. Detroit executives scoffed at it and didn't listen to the field and engineering levels where a profound respect had developed for the adversary.

During the Vietnam War, Washington told the field commanders what Washington wanted to hear. Similarly, Detroit executives told the engineering departments what they should think and the customers what they should want. So, Detroit executives continued to ignore the engineers' mail, the complaints of customers about warranties and the reports from Hertz that the quality of Japanese cars was greater than that of GM or Ford. They had contempt for their customers as well as their foreign competitors.

As in Vietnam, the reality became obscure. What neither Detroit nor Washington could see, I think, was a form of Asian nationalism. In Vietnam, the expression of it was political, attaining dignity by driving out the foreigners. In Japan, the aim was economic, attaining dignity by giving ordinary citizens, who in the past had lived under brutal conditions, a good job, a decent place to live, a good diet and a chance for their children to have a better education.

Detroit's Tet Offensive

The Tet Offensive opened our eyes in Vietnam. The auto industry's Tet came in 1979 when, in the immortal words of Lee Iacocca, "The Shah of Iran left town."

When the Shah left Teheran in 1979 and the price of oil quadrupled, Americans were caught with big cars while the Japanese produced all the small cars. Even more important, the Japanese had by then slowly and painstakingly built up a reputation for quality among customers and auto dealers. Detroit executives didn't believe this was true until their backs were against the wall. Then, when their people began to break down the cars and compare them, they were stunned at how much better the Japanese really were.

Then they finally paid attention, Detroit understood that these unlikely challengers had come up with a very good system of production. In terms of manufacturing, the Japanese had become the true children of Henry Ford while the top people at our companies were now lawyers and business school graduates. The car men had all been replaced by financial men.

The "manufacturing men" at places like Ford, GM and Chrysler had become second class citizens. They got the smallest bonuses, the worst jobs, the smallest salaries. They had been to the wrong schools and they wore double-knit polyester jackets. The engineers lacked panache, but the people who ran the company could barely change a tire.

America's Reckoning

We are talking about the end of the "American Century" —the oil century which began with the first Model-T and ended with import quotas against Japanese subcompacts. We are talking about a more limited notion of American power, one in which we are still immensely powerful but in which our power has to be more carefully used.

We are not now, and no one else will ever be, as powerful and rich as America was from 1945–1975. We are now living in a new, unsentimental age for which we are not particularly well-suited. We are entering a highly competitive world in which knowledge and human resources, not military might and natural resources, will be the dominant aspects of power. Applied brain power, as exemplified coming of the Japanese, is more important than god-given natural resources.

The Shared Middle Class

It is a mistake to believe that the high-water mark of what the Japanese can do well is automobiles. There is a real hunger in Japan, a belief in the primacy of education and a lack of waste that is admirable. They are a part of the culture of adversity. From now on, America's culture of affluence is going to live in an age in which all kinds of other nations from the culture of adversity aspire to, and will attain, middle-class status.

That means America must shed a good deal of its arrogance. We must overcome the Pavlovian response that when something goes wrong it is the other guys who are somehow unfair. But the other guys aren't unfair in the way they flood engineers onto the factory floor. The other guys aren't unfair in the way they turn out twice as many engineers as we do. The other guys aren't unfair in making sure that elementary school kids can master their own language and have basic mathematical skills.

On Leadership

We haven't accepted the reckoning yet. I think people understand in a visceral sense that something terribly important has happened. They are desperate for someone who can honestly explain what has gone wrong and how it might be turned around. But I get no sense of leadership these days.

Although the problem we are dealing with here is not ideological, but societal, I must say that Ronald Reagan still sounds like one of those beer commercials aired during the 1984 Olympics about how America has come back.

But America hasn't come back. And the problem is not just in autos, but across the whole society. The average American family still does not realize that if its offspring do not study hard they are going to lose a job to someone in Korea or Japan. We're in trouble as long as the status of "nerd" is assigned to a male child of 15 in an average high school who gets good grades.

One of Ronald Reagan's big problems is that he does not think the Vietnam War was a mistake. He thinks we should have won. He does not have any respect for the Vietnamese and why they won. Failing that, it is very hard for him to learn anything much from that war or from other reality checks on America's sense of itself. He is obsessed with the things that might have obsessed a president in the mid-1950s and still acts as if the greatest danger to us is the Soviet Union. But the Russians can't even truck tomatoes from Tblisi to Moscow and are being surpassed by Korea in industrial capacity! We place so much of our psychological energy into thinking about Nicaragua, a nation with two elevators, while the Japanese are building a supercomputer and the quintessential American car, the Mustang, may soon be made by Mazda.

That kind of leadership is a sign that America is not tempering itself, not reading its mail. We need to learn the lessons of our new challenge and not be pulled down by the ghosts of the past.

U.S. AND JAPAN RELATIONSHIP: ECONOMIC ACTIVITIES[5]

Thank you Dan, president, distinguished guests, ladies and gentlemen. It is my great honor and pleasure to be invited to this notable luncheon of Ann Arbor Rotary Club to which I owe so much for overwhelming hospitality and timely guidance. I will someday repay in the Japanese yen.

Let me first express my heart-felt thanks to Mr. and Mrs. Dan Balback for their kindness and help extended to my family. Without their help, my one-year-old daughter might have lost her life when she had a seizure in February.

It was around 9:30 p.m. when she fell into a fit of convulsions because of an extremely high fever and stopped breathing. Her face quickly turned ashen and her lips purple. My wife shouted, "Call an ambulance!" I rushed to the phone only to find out I didn't know what number to call. The only number I could think of was 110 and 119. Those are the numbers for the police and an ambulance in Japan, respectively. Out of desperation, I called Dan and it was his wife, Barbara, who told me to calm down and dial 911.

Within minutes, we got two fire engines, two police patrol cars and an ambulance. Our daughter was fit as a fiddle on the following day while my wife and I felt as if we were 10 years older. I'm sure some of you have gone through the same experience.

Despite such unexpected happenings, it's been a wonderful year both as a journalist in residence and a Rotary scholar.

I'm not sure whether I've been a great goodwill ambassador as Rotary International expected me to be, but I've tried my best. Thanks to Rotary and the University of Michigan, I've had numerous occasions to speak in public on a wide range of topics such

[5]Reprint of a speech by Seiichi Kamise, Rotary Journalism Fellow, University of Michigan. *Vital Speeches of the Day*. Jl. 15, '88. Reprinted with permission.

as education, trade, cultural differences and U.S.-Japanese relations.

My comments were not always soothing or pleasant to the Americans but the American audience responded to both good news and bad news magnanimously. It is my conviction that for successful cross-cultural communication, one should not expect good news alone or bad news only.

When the Soviet leader called President Reagan, a White House official rushed to the President and said, "Good news Mr. President, General Secretary Gorbachev is calling to say he is in favor of free speech. The bad news is he is calling collect."

Since this is my last scheduled speaking commitment in Ann Arbor, I'd like to share with you some of my observations and thoughts on the U.S.-Japanese relations today.

When I first came to the United States nearly 20 years ago, few Americans showed real interest in Japan. Even President Johnson mistakenly called a Japanese prime minister Prime Minister Shastri, who was of course the prime minister of India at that time.

Today, Japan has invaded not only your living room and garage but also your consciousness. I'm pleased that today I don't have to emphasize Japan is not merely Fujiyama and Geisha girls or sushi and sake.

But at the same time, I'm deeply disturbed by the fact that our two nations' relations have been narrowly focused on trade and business issues in recent years in disregard of our rich and diversified cultural traits and shared aspirations for freedom, justice and democracy. No matter how important and urgent the trade issue might be, to focus solely on that dimension of bilateral ties would be detrimental to our over-all relations in the long run.

According to a recent Japanese newspaper survey on the most favorite foreign country among Japanese, the United States ranked first with about 40 percent followed by China with some 20 percent, while the Soviet Union got only 4 percent. Why?

The answer is respect and friendship. Americans who came over to Japan when Japan opened its doors to the West in the mid-19th century included many outstanding scholars, missionaries, educators, technical experts who brought with them an enormous variety of American culture. Even during the post-war U.S. occupation of Japan, the Americans brought not just troops and tanks but also their culture.

By contrast, the relations between Japan and the Soviet Union have centered on a single dimension of military conflict over the past 100 or so years and there has been no room for lasting friendship to develop between the two peoples.

I, as a frequent visitor to your country, understand American frustration over Japan's recent economic success. When a revolution occurred in a Middle East country, the heads of all branches of foreign companies were arrested and sentenced to death as anti-revolutionaries. Prior to their execution, they were asked if they had last wishes. The French businessman said he wants to sing La Marseillaise, the French national anthem, before he dies and his wish was granted. The next, a Japanese businessman, said, "I want to give my last lecture on Japanese management." Upon hearing this, the American businessman shouted, "You'd better shoot me first, I'm sick of it."

Americans often complain of trade imbalances with Japan, but have you really tried hard to export your goods to Japan as earnestly as when you sent the Apollo spaceship to the moon? When General Electric first tried to sell its refrigerators to Japan, the company found their products were too large for Japanese houses. Some GE executives asked Japan to build larger houses. Some ill-informed Americans openly claimed Japan is keeping its streets narrow in order to prevent the sales of big American automobiles there.

Columbia University Professor Gerald L. Curtis recently wrote in the *New York Times* that much American criticism of Japan is ill-informed and little more than a convenient excuse for not facing up to "our own problems."

French poet Paul Valery said, "No nation blames itself for its own unhappiness." Little has been more pernicious in international politics than excessive righteousness.

I have observed many American businessman take it for granted that their Japanese counterparts stationed in the United States speak English, while they don't bother to learn the Japanese language when they are sent to the other side of the Pacific.

Learning English is not easy for the Japanese. For many Japanese it is extremely difficult to distinguish L from R and there is a joke about it.

A Japanese old man who has lived many years in California one day had some trouble with his eyes and went to see a doctor. Thanks to long years of hard work, he is now rich and drives a

Lincoln. After an examination, the doctor told the man, "You have a cataract." The old man, surprised, said "No, no, doctor. I have a Rincorn."

Shocked by his poor English, the doctor then asked, "Haven't you ever studied English?" The old man, standing tall, answered, "Of course, I went to U.C.R.A." When the doctor blamed the university for failing to provide him with adequate English language education, the old man angrily said, "Don't speak like that about my school. I want to tell you where to go. But it's too difficult to pronounce."

As for defense, why can't Americans be content with the fact that Japan has become a stable economic power and the showcase of democracy in Asia without becoming a military power? Students of history know well that economic powers have inevitably become military powers. Given Japan's track record with cars, TVs, VCRs and computer chips, it's not an unrealistic thought that one of Japan's industrial giants may take a unilateral lead in armament output. Some U.S. lawmakers publicly demand Japan to boost its defense spending and revise its constitution which renounces military forces. But isn't demanding a sovereign state to rewrite its constitution a presumptuous interference in the nation's domestic affairs? Japan indeed spends more each year on entertainment than it does on defense and it's not bad. No country with such priorities is likely to march off to reconquer the Philippines and Korea.

Thirdly on U.S. foreign policy. Since the end of World War II, Washington has often taken unilateral self-willed policies vis-à-vis Japan. For example, the United States virtually forced Japan to adopt the "peace" constitution prohibiting rearming of Japan, while it's now pressing Japan to shoulder military burdens in Asia. The Americans often innocently ask the Japanese, "Who made you such pacifists?"

While urging Japan to collaborate with Washington's "China containment policy," President Nixon suddenly visited Beijing and shook hands with Chairman Mao and Premier Chou. It was a clear violation of the U.S.-Japanese communique which stipulates the two nations should hold prior consultations in case of an important change in their Asian policy.

By the same token, President Carter shocked the Japanese and Koreans as well by unilaterally announcing the withdrawal of part of U.S. troops from South Korea. Despite all the humiliating happenings, Japan has remained loyal to the United States.

Please don't misunderstand me. I'm not a die-hard nationalist. There is no doubt Japan owes tremendously to the United States for its post-war rehabilitation and it should not forget that. But as Arthur Schlesinger Jr. said, "the assumption that other nations have legitimate traditions, values and rights of their own is the beginning of a true morality of states."

Year ago, I heard a story at the United Nations. When Japanese, Roman and Arab princesses are taking shower together, a male thief sneaked in. The Japanese princess flushed and immediately covered her underbelly with a towel. The Roman princess, saying "Oh, My!," covered her breast, while the Arab princess, uttering "What a shame!," covered her face with her hands. Who can say one is more sophisticated or barbaric than others?

The United States once looked down upon Japan as a copycat. But please remember imitation is the sincerest form of flattery, and when a copy excels the original, it's no longer a copy. The automobile was first invented by a Frenchman but it was Henry Ford who improved it and made it a great means of transportation for you and me.

I am a fan of the United States and American people. It is my impression that your Founding Fathers were hard workers with modesty and a strong sense of responsibility, who loved freedom but valued prudence. Now I am very much disheartened to see the country I admire so much is becoming an undisciplined society with rampant permissiveness and political degradation. The United States, it seems to me, is filled with DIS-culture. Discomfort, displeasure, disillusion, dissatisfaction, and distemper.

Benjamin Franklin said, "Content makes a poor man rich and discontent makes a rich man poor." In this respect, the United States today seems to be a very poor country.

I still remember I was deeply impressed when I was young to learn that Woodrow Wilson became the president of the United States from the president of Princeton via the governorship of New Jersey. It is utterly unthinkable that president of Tokyo University could become prime minister of Japan.

I strongly felt Japan should follow the United States in intellectualization of politicians. But it seems to be that the U.S. politics have been much Japanized. When I look at the faces of recent U.S. presidents—Johnson, Nixon, Ford, Carter, Reagan and Dukakis or Bush—I'm convinced there is something wrong with Darwinism.

An influential U.S. congressman, who attended a Tokyo conference aimed at discussing bilateral relations from a global perspective, shocked the Japanese delegation by demanding Japan to buy more coal from his constituency.

The United States of America I respect is a country of vision and a magnanimous people with fortitude, strong commitment to democracy and decency, and a good sense of humor even in times of crises.

In early 1980s when the U.S. auto industry was hit hard by Japanese imports, an American businessman told me a story about a Chrysler dealer. The dealer, depressed by sagging sales, began drinking heavily and soon his wife and children left him. One day when he was rubbing his whisky bottle with a shaking hand as usual, a big white smoke and a giant genie suddenly came out of the bottle. You know Aladdin and the Wonderful Lamp.

The mean-looking genie told the Chrysler dealer, "Thank you for helping me out of the bottle. I will grant you one wish."

The dealer immediately shouted, "Please give me an import dealership!"

When the genie and the smoke disappeared, the dealer found himself right in the middle of Tokyo, selling Chryslers.

Years ago, on the final round of British Open Golf tournament, Tom Watson and British golfer Nick Faldo were competing neck-and-neck. When Watson was about to putt on a crucial hole, a small child in the gallery suddenly let out a cry, an unthinkable bad behavior in the country of ladies and gentlemen. Watson could stare at the boy or complain to officials. Instead, he just smiled and said, "He must be Nick's fan." Then taking a deep breath, he rolled in a birdie putt.

Hedrick Smith of NYT wrote in his latest book *The Power Game* that Americans are a game-loving people preoccupied with winning and losing. But bilateral trade deficit is not like the final score in a football game, because economic activities never end. One of the basic principles of economics is that both sides gain from an exchange.

For the rest of this century and beyond, divorce between U.S. and Japan is economically impossible, militarily impractical and politically unthinkable.

If the situation gets really out of hand, the United States can sink Japan in 20 seconds. But the U.S. itself will go down two days later.

It is, I believe, the urgent and momentous task for both nations to expand their relations to wider fields—not just government-to-government or business-to-business but also people-to-people as Rotary does—and promote true understanding of each other.

For the issue among friends is not how they can use each other but how they can serve each other.

Thank you very much.

THE UNITED STATES–JAPAN PARTNERSHIP:
THE WAVE OF THE PRESENT[6]

In late November, 1988, as we prepare for the passing of a President from office and the passing of an aged Emperor from life, we should, from the standpoint of relations between the United States and Japan, take even more notice of the passing from the public arena of two remarkable politicians, one American, one Japanese, both of whom exemplify the qualities of vision and character required today of leaders in the world's most important partnership. These two men are Ambassador and former Senator Mike Mansfield of the United States and Representative and former Prime Minister Takeo Miki, for 51 years a democratic parliamentarian for Japan. You may not have noticed the retirement of Mike Mansfield at age 85 or the death of Takeo Miki this month at the age of 81. Neither was flamboyant or given to undemocratic manipulation of media "sound bites" or the employment of political "spin artists" to distort his political persona in the manner of recent American campaign politics. Both were quiet men in high office; in different settings, both were powerful. They affected the lives of vast numbers of humans in a positive way over a long period of time.

Mike Mansfield was an instructor in East Asian history in Montana, a place where mountains and space can ease the development of large-mindedness. Mike Mansfield used his teaching

[6]Reprint of a speech by Lawrence W. Beer, Coordinator, East Asian Studies and F. M. Kirby Professor of Civil Rights, Lafayette College. *Vital Speeches of the Day.* Ja. 1, '89. Reprinted with permission.

skills well in the labyrinthine hallways of American congressional politics, serving as Senate Majority Leader for 16 years, longer than anyone in history. He also held the post of Ambassador to Japan longer than any predecessor, for 11 years. During his tenure, frictions between the United States and Japan have been recurrent, with many in both Japan and America coming to the stunned realization that Japan, if not necessarily "number one," had surpassed the United States in important areas of technological, educational, economic and criminological performance. Ambassador Mansfield has contrasted with those aggrieved American politicians, industrialists, union leaders, journalists, and academicians who have pointed to the mote in Japan's eye each time an area of Japanese superiority has come to light. What we might call "the Mansfield camp" has reacted with more measured moderation. Ambassador Mansfield has been respectfully straightforward, not petulant, in defending effectively America's interests in Japan, while admitting our economic foibles in a blunt and balanced way. For this, he has earned the respect and affection of the Japanese people. More than most political figures whose names are bruited about in the media, Mike Mansfield deserves the appellation of "statesman" and "patriot" at a time when America's well-being depends not on ludicrous pretensions to permanent world primacy, but on cool-eyed contemplation of immediate and long-term national and global needs.

Similar in his patient, quiet and persistent style was Takeo Miki, a name relatively few Americans are likely to remember. In the late 1930s, Mr. Miki's was one of those noble but ineffectual voices in Japanese politics preaching democracy and moderation, along with the equality of all non-white and white peoples, rather than the popular militarism and extreme nationalism of the times. He studied at both Meiji University in Tokyo and the University of Southern California at Berkeley. Like Mr. Mansfield with his knowledge of East Asia, so Mr. Miki comprehended better than most of his contemporaries the bewildering complexities of the United States. As a holder of cabinet positions in postwar Japan, he was known as "Mr. Clean" for his unfailing efforts for reform and ethics in public life. As Prime Minister in 1974, he had his predecessor, Kakuei Tanaka, arrested for political corruption. Unlike some of America's top political criminals, Tanaka has been tried and convicted under democratic law. Unlike most of his peers, Mr. Miki was able to speak English, the world's diplomatic language. To summarize his career, he remained a model of commitment to democracy, honest politics, peace, and the building of partnership with the United States.

The competent, principled and quiet tone of these two gentlemen is precisely what seems appropriate for the continued strengthening of bonds between Japan and the United States. In "Hamlet," Polonius tells Laertes: "The friends thou hast, and their adoption tried, grapple them to thy soul with hoops of steel." The relationship between Japan and the United States has been well tried for over forty years, and one may say that "hoops of steel" of friendship have been formed between many Japanese and American citizens; but it is dangerous to confuse friendship with partnership or ordinary relations between two nation states. Individuals become friends, not nation states. The U.S.-Japan partnership works because we are bound by the "hoops of steel" of long-term common interests.

That our cultures are radically different does not imply less commonality of interest. Cultural affinity between two nations can obscure the fact that governments hard-headedly appraise their respective national self-interests and act accordingly. Diplomacy may not be, as cynics say, doing the meanest things to other countries in the nicest way, but neither is it about friendship. Cultural affinity may ease the development of individual friendships; but great affinity can co-exist with extreme antagonism, as between North and South Korea, between Taiwan and China, between Germany of the 1930s and the rest of Europe. Great cultural affinities can be found between Canada and the United States. But the Canadians are voting in elections today for Canada's interests, not ours, with respect to the free trade treaty and leadership. When two governments represent radically different cultures, as do the United States and Japan, there may be less danger of rhetorically confusing friendship with correct international relations or an international partnership. On the other hand, I would submit that frictions within our partnership are ultimately traceable less to economic, political or military factors than to problems of intercultural communication.

My thesis here is that the United States–Japan relationship is a preculiarly important partnership warranting its designation as "the wave of the present" in world affairs. Whether it is "the wave of the future" is not clear; but it can be. This partnership is now the most influential bi-national relationship in the world, with the proviso that in military terms the U.S.-U.S.S.R. pairing has most clout. In the very limited military sense, those two countries are "superpowers," but the very term "superpower" seems otherwise useless and misleading for purposes of describing international power, because most elements of power are non-military in nature, and because the emerging world structure seems to meld together multinational economics with omni-national interdependence.

The United States–Japan partnership is not a bilateral relationship with an autonomous, isolated existence; rather, it affects the political, economic, ecological and social life of the entire Pacific Basin and the world, and thus carries with it both heavy global responsibilities and opportunities for joint leadership. World institutions of government and economy seem to be passing through one of their few periods of seminal exchange. Japan's 1947 Constitution is one of only about 20 in the world that were ratified by 1950. Well over 100 of the present 165 single-document national constitutions have been ratified since 1970; an unprecedented and increasing commonality of governmental forms characterizes current politico-legal trends. Refinements of law and structure to fit each country's cultural matrix seem likely to lend stability to states in most regions within a mere half century. Economic thought and practice reflect no comparable consensus on either alternative ideals or the real. Currency exchange rates are unsettled. National debts in a good many important countries, including the U.S., are at or near catastrophic levels. The shibboleths and slogans of "free trade" and "protectionism," "big government" or small, have not been squared with any carefully defined outlines for the design of a new world economic order.

The term "security" no longer means only a nation's military security, except to the myopically uninformed. "National security" within the U.S.-Japan partnership can now be properly explicated only with informed awareness of "*world security*." What do I mean by "world security" in this context? Of course an absence of war must be included as a goal; but even war is no longer primarily a matter of relations between military forces. In 1987, roughly 70 percent of war deaths were of non-combatant men, women and children, representing a dramatic rise in percentage in only a few decades. But "world security" requires much more of the Japan-U.S. partnership besides working for peace and the protection of war victims. Due to their unequaled capacities, they should lead in seeking solutions to such global problems as hunger, unmanageable national debt, and a deteriorating ecology.

The Global Hunger Project estimates that 35,000 people die each day, over 12.5 million each year, from starvation. About 75 percent of these victims are children, and thus politically voiceless. Chronic hunger now kills more people each year than all known major famines of the past twenty years. Moreover, the ecological health of the atmosphere and water supplies of the earth are at risk; and known extractable mineral resources are rapidly dwindling. The U.S.-Japan partnership should lead in efforts to find alternatives and to maintain a healthy ozone layer. Already it is clear that temperatures will rise within a few decades to levels seriously affecting climate and living conditions in large regions of the planet. Unfortunately, related problems of humankind are sometimes perfunctorily reported and casually dismissed or even covered up by political and business interests; the unpleasant truth must out, especially as a preoccupation of such partnerships as that of the U.S. and Japan. Fossil fuel consumption, the rapid industrial development of more nations, desertification of large areas, and deforestation are now remaking the earth's surface more inexorably than any influence since the ice age. In addition, if the rate of consumption throughout the planet were at American and Japanese rates, the known supplies of resources would be used up within months. A mature partnership must face up to the burdens of world leadership. Unfortunately, the 1980s has been a "decade of denials" in the United States, denial of both national and international problems while sitting in the dark enjoying the warm glow of a bright, friendly presidential face. For her part, Japan has clung to a defensive ethnic separatism, moving only at glacial pace to assume planetary responsibilities attendant to power. More than any alternative pair or group of nations, the United States–Japan partnership must seize the time and lead.

What does "partnership" mean? The term derives from law; so nothing so wishy-washy as friendship is in its root meaning. "Partners" are joint principals united by a contract in a business. More broadly, partnership is a relationship of close cooperation over time in which each party, because of persistent shared interests, assumes specific and joint rights and responsibilities. What are the narrowly national and broadly international interests involved in the United States–Japan partnership?

First, the two countries share a living commitment to constitutional democracy; freedom and individual rights under law, democratic elections, and government with divided and limited power really do matter to both Japanese and Americans. So the partnership unites Western and non-Western models of democratic government and law, with Japan in the more influential European civil law tradition and the United States in the English common law tradition. Both countries have relatively serious weaknesses in the protection of democracy, quality of life, and human rights; but many public and private figures in both nations work tirelessly to improve the quality of democratic life, and both are in the upper fifth of countries when judged by constitutionalist principles. Leaders in both are routinely elected without political upheaval.

A second element bonding the partnership is the unique relationship under the aegis of the 1960 United States–Japan Treaty for Mutual Security and Cooperation. Article 9 of the 1947 Constitution of Japan (*Nihonkoku Kempo*) forbids Japan from having normal armed forces or using military force against other nations. Article 9 acts as a powerful check on Japan's military spending, nuclear weaponry, defense research, munitions industry, dispatch of military personnel abroad, possession of offensive weaponry, and general approach to the solution of international disputes. Japan's quasi-pacifism under Article 9 is historically unique and constitutes Japan's only significant contribution to the world's tradition of constitutional thought and institutions. The Japanese public overwhelmingly supports the Constitution in general and in particular Article 9, and does not seem to believe that Japan should resort to international force under any circumstances. However, polls indicate the citizenry also approves of the existence of the "Self-Defence Forces" (*Jieitai*) at a geopolitically modest level of less than 250,000 in a region where even the smallest countries, such as Taiwan and North Korea, have twice that military capacity. Most of Japan's constitutional lawyers consider the Self-Defense Forces unconstititutional. So sensitive are many Japanese still to the pre-1945 horrors of antidemocratic militarism that it was 1988 before Japan sent its first two Foreign Ministry officials (not military personnel) abroad to assist the United Nations on site with the administration of peace settlements in Afghanistan and the Iran-Iraq War. In place of military spending proportionate to economic power, Japan chooses to fulfill its international responsibilities now as a leading aid donor. Japan has recently taken the lead position by committing itself to over $50 billion in ODA (Official Development Assistance) to less fortunate countries between 1988 and 1992.

Paradoxically, even with Japan's constraints on the military, it has one of the largest military budgets in the world, because the spending ceiling of 1% of GNP represents much money in a huge economy. Although some Americans, on limited information, claim that Japan takes a "free ride" under the U.S. nuclear umbrella, that is factually inaccurate. The two governments have generally been in agreement on Article 9 questions, though the Reagan administration has seemed to favor increased military expenditures in a way troubling not only to many Japanese and other Asians with sharp memories of World War II, but also to some defense and diplomatic officials within the American government. As the influential *Asahi* newspaper eloquently editorialized on Constitution Day this year, there is indeed a clash between two notions of what constitutes "common sense" in Japan's international affairs, militarized foreign policies or powerful inhibitions on military development and resort to violence. No large country has a more peaceful and successful record than Japan since 1945. The U.S.-Japan partnership has worked well for both countries in the defense area.

The third element in the partnership is economic relations, which is too often equated with "real" U.S.-Japan relations, due to shallowness and the dramatic visibility of some related successes and problems. Indeed, our overseas trade is the largest in history; economics *is* important. The fact that Japan's economic success may well be premised on its continuous democratic stability, rather than vice-versa, is often utterly ignored. Also seriously underplayed is the centrality of an extraordinary cultural interaction and a wide culture gap in explanations of both the glories and the frictions in our economic partnership over the past 35 to 40 years. It is the great good fortune of both countries, as the two leading powers, that they are enmeshed in a multi-dimensional partnership and not just an economic relationship. Because culture gap is such a key factor in frictions, subtle interdisciplinary analysis of context must often be combind with detailed, sophisticated consideration of technicalities of law, government, technology and business processes for balance communication to occur. That requires patient, open-minded study on both sides. Japanese knowledge of the United States, both in general and in technical areas, is at once more extensive and more widely diffused than American knowledge of Japan. Typically, Japanese businesses much more carefully study potential foreign markets than their American counterparts before attempting entry. The American side has more often been characterized by an overweening hubris, an apparent assumption on the part of businessmen, financiers, government personnel, and even some intellectuals that the United States has appropriately defined human economic structures and values as well as the rules of the economic game for the planet Earth. On the Japanese side, although the government intervenes less than the U.S. government on behalf of failing industries and in research and development, though Japan's tariffs are now lower than American tariffs, and though far more Japanese are well-informed on American affairs than Americans about Japan, non-tariff barriers and a distinctively complex distribution system restrict foreign market entry, and resentful incomprehension of the other's position is recurrent among Japanese as among Americans. The fierce nationalism on both sides may sometimes be a factor, but should not be confused with intercultural incomprehension.

The economic reasons for Japanese protectionism may well have evaporated in recent decades, as they are in the process of doing in our trade with South Korea, Taiwan, Hong Kong, Singapore and other Newly Industrialized Countries. The United States has had justifiable complaints to bring against Japan and others who have benefitted from our relatively open and immense marketplace while not opening as wide their own markets to American interests. But we tend to overlook that in size and openness, the United States market is not a world model, but a uniquely deviant case; we also tend to exaggerate the utility of "bashing" our trade partners. It won't right the trade imbalance, and the tone of the bashing sometimes suggests that the U.S. is not only the self-appointed legitimate arbiter for all, but is also a poor loser when other nations have applied new technologies more widely than Americans, as in the steel and auto industries. Whatever Japan has done since the 1960s in response to our demands, we have found new cause for the trade imbalance.

Professor James Morley well summarizes the sequence:

When this problem first appeared, the American charge was that Japan was unfairly protecting its market with tariffs and quotas. Since about

1965 Japan has restructured its tariffs until its average is lower than that of the United States. Quotas have been abandoned on many items though not on all . . . (such as a few) agricultural products. . . . We then found unfair competition in the American market, charging Japan with paying unfairly low wages, subsidizing its export industries, or "dumping" its goods abroad unfairly in order to gain unwarranted market shares. We went after threatening industries and still do. Then it was the exchange rate, pegged at a level that made Japanese exports unfairly cheap and American exports unfairly expensive. The rate has been brought down from 360 yen to the dollar to roughly 130 yen [123 yen at time of writing] to the dollar. Then we turned our attention back to the Japanese market to assault its inspection procedures and other internal restrictions. Now some Americans are complaining about the unfairness of Japan's having social values and institutions different from our own. . . .

What are we to do? What are the Japanese to do? Surely not play an endlessly bruising game of economic and political football to a scoreless tie. It will do no good to bash for bashing's sake. House Majority Leader Thomas Foley, commenting on the strained communications attending the shift of relative power from the U.S. to Japan, recently said:

I have noticed from time to time that in the United States the coverage of Japanese affairs is so ineffective and insufficient that it keeps the American public, including members of Congress and the business community, ignorant of positive developments occurring in Japan. On the other hand, the Japanese public is often given intense coverage of everything that happens in the United States, particularly those negative developments. . . . But I would hope that we in the United States could have greater coverage of events in Japan and that perhaps the Japanese press would give greater attention to *positive* developments in the United States.

As yet, the political and educational leadership of the United States, and thus the media leadership, has not considered it important that education should include coverage of Japan and other Asian countries. Relatively very few of the thousands of American colleges and universities have even one well-trained Japan specialist on their faculties. To train a professional Japanologist can take twice as long as preparing a professor in Western learning. Given the failure of American higher education to concern itself with the Japanese partnership and world security, few opportunities for educational employment await the newly minted Ph.D. in Japanese Studies or other areas of Asian Studies; so very few take up the challenge to meet the national need. Perhaps the demise of the United States will be attended by an ever-firmer conviction that, as the song goes, "We are the world." Or perhaps the schools of law, medicine, engineering and business, the too-technocratic and thus less-respected components of the traditional university community, will take the lead in requiring careful study of Japanese culture and politics precisely because it provides the most needed, the most practical preparation for those who would succeed professionally in the international future.

The United States–Japan partnership serves the political, military, economic and cultural interests of both countries. I would close by pointing to an additional dimension that may be of immense import: I would contend that this partnership is the most important bi-lateral partnership between two great powers of radically different culture in the history of the world. The centuries of Western domination, like the short decades of American primacy, are coming to an end. In past relationships, equality of status was not achieved by countries of radically different culture; they often, as in the case of 19th-century Europe and China, had fundamentally incompatible understandings of what "international relations" might mean. By now, the territorial nation state has been accepted almost universally as the primary unit for international legal and political relations. However, this world system's history is short; and even where political ideologies do not divide major powers, culture gaps do and will continue to divide deeply.

Japan's ascendancy to world power status over the past thirty years may mark an early stage in the emergence of non-white peoples in Asia, Africa, and Latin America to a position of power parity with ethnic Europeans on the planet Earth. Among all countries, the United States has the closest relationship with Japan, perhaps Japan's only partnership. To be the much-needed appropriate model for future partnerships between great powers of radically different culture, the United States and Japan must take each other with deadly seriousness and respect, mutually accepting the legitimacy of their different social and economic structures and value emphases while reciprocally yielding small modifications for fairness, all within a shared framework of concern for constitutional democracy and world security. This effort to encounter and work with the radically other culture so essential to education today cannot but broaden perspectives; but a partnership will function well only with honesty about the often intractable intercultural communication problems. In efforts at mature partnership, we need to study each other much more; but even more essential to problem-solution are the qualities of Mike Mansfield and Takeo Miki: large-minded patience, respect, persistence, and an underlying trust in the partner's good faith. With those, the United States–Japan partnership will surely be part of the wave of the future.

U.S.-JAPANESE RELATIONS IN FOCUS[7]

Dr. Sigur [Gaston J. Sigur, Jr., Assistant Secretary for East Asian and Pacific Affairs] is sorry he could not be with you, but I am delighted to be here today on his behalf to speak to you about our most important bilateral relationship: that between the United States and Japan. For two nations to be so closely intertwined as the United States and Japan today, despite dissimilar histories and a bitter war still within memory, is unprecedented. It is difficult to understand how we could have forged, during the period following World War II, such a remarkably durable alliance.

We have built this alliance over 40 years upon shared values and extensive mutual interests and on those things we need from each other. Our relationship is now deep and multidimensional. And it is important that we keep the many dimensions in mind as we confront difficult individual issues. For while the United States and Japan continue to be close partners, both in the economic arena and in terms of international political and security cooperation, it is also true that headlines about our relations these days more often than not highlight trade frictions between the two nations. Someone once said good news is no news. Still I would like to accentuate the positive, without overlooking the sore points, to bring our relationship with Japan into better focus.

Japan's extraordinary economic ascendance and our own trade and budget deficits have led many to see Japan as a hostile economic competitor and the United States as in danger of losing its preeminence as the economic and political leader of the free world. This view overlooks the many benefits our relationship

[7]Reprint of a speech by William Clark, Jr., Deputy Assistant Secretary for East Asian and Pacific Affairs. *Department of State Bulletin*, Ap. '88.

with Japan brings to us and strays from the traditional American spirit of competition. We Americans are competitors. We believe competition—open and fair competition—makes us excel. That philosophy is the basis of our policy toward Japan. We are determined to bring our trade with Japan into a more balanced equilibrium, to promote our own economic interests, and to maintain our strong political and security relationship.

Japan's selection of a new prime minister last November and his visit to Washington this January provided the opportunity for a fresh look at our bilateral relationship. Ambassador [to Japan] Mike Mansfield has called it the most important bilateral relationship in the world, bar none. During his January visit to Washington, Prime Minister Takeshita, a most experienced and capable political leader, reaffirmed his view that Japan's relations with the United States are the cornerstone of Japan's foreign policy. President Reagan emphasized Japan's role as America's most important partner and ally in the Pacific. Let me touch on the reasons why the United States and Japan should view each other as close allies, as well as tough competitors.

Economic Ties

At about $115 billion year, two-way trade between our countries is larger than the gross national product of most nations. The United States is Japan's number one export market, absorbing 36% of Japan's exports, and Japan is our number one supplier. In return Japan receives about 11% of U.S. exports, including $6.8 billion in foodstuffs last year, making Japan by far the U.S. farmer's best customer. In fact Japan bought more goods from the United States than did West Germany, France, and Italy combined. We estimate that the $27.5 billion in goods Japan bought from us last year sustained over 700,000 American jobs.

Within Japan we are the number one foreign investor at $11 billion. American firms such as IBM, Xerox, and Schick hold significant market positions in Japan. Affiliates of U.S. multinationals had $80 billion in sales, imported $3 billion in goods from the United States, and had $2 billion in net income in Japan in 1985. And right from Georgia, the Coca Cola Company took an estimated 60% share of the Japanese soft drink market that year.

In the United States, Japanese direct investment is rising dramatically, although Japan is only the number three foreign investor behind the United Kingdom and the Netherlands, with $24 billion in direct investments. In 1985 Japanese firms employed 208,000 Americans and exported $23 billion in goods. Since then, to use the auto industry as an important example, each of the major Japanese companies has built plants here, bought more U.S.-made parts, and begun implementing plans to export cars back to Japan.

In 1986 we estimate that Japanese investors put $65 billion into U.S. money markets. Interest on our budget deficit would increase if Japanese funds did not flow in. The United States is the Japanese investment country of choice. In 1987 Japan's net overseas investment increased to an astounding total of $137 billion. Japan exports more capital overseas in global investments than it earns from its current account surplus.

Since 1981 our trade imbalance with Japan has tripled, from $18 billion to $60 billion. The U.S. global trade deficit quadrupled from $40 billion to about $170 billion over the same period. There are barriers to U.S. exports in Japan, and these must be dismantled. But the imbalance with Japan is a symptom of broader macroeconomic forces. We have a global trade imbalance problem, as well as a bilateral one.

We have worked hard with Japan to reduce these external imbalances—Japan's surplus and the U.S. deficit—while maintaining non-inflationary growth. The most visible aspect of this cooperation has been the appreciation of the yen from 265 to 130 per dollar since 1985. This has helped boost U.S. exports and helped U.S. firms win market share in Japan and at home.

At the same time, new purchases of foreign assets became economical for Japanese overseas investors. When converted to dollars at the new rate, Japan's per capita GNP now exceeds our own. Foreign travel and imported goods are great bargains now for most Japanese. And the physical volume of Japan's exports has declined along with the yen value of those exports. Growth now comes from Japan's domestic economy, not exports.

Japan's global current account surplus, which was $87 billion in 1987, and our bilateral trade imbalance are projected to decline this year. Japan is shifting from export-led to domestic-led growth policies to aid the reduction further. Japan had negative net external growth in 1987 and strong domestic expansion and is expected to have 3.7% real GNP growth in the fiscal year which ends in March.

Already, by taking measures to spur private consumption, housing investment, and public works, the Japanese Government has reduced reliance on export-led growth. An influential study, the Maekawa report issued in April 1986, contains a blueprint for alleviating the Japanese surplus and putting Japan on course for economic growth in harmony with the needs of its economic partners. It has been embraced by Japan's business leadership and supported by Prime Minister Takeshita, but only partially implemented. We encourage Japan to follow through on its recommendations.

In sum, our economic policy toward Japan has as its central goal the expansion of trade, not the limiting of it. We seek removal of individual trade barriers. We encourage appropriate structural and macroeconomic reforms in Japan. And we seek to cooperate with Japan in promoting the success of the new GATT [General Agreement on Tariffs and Trade] trade round, where we both aim to establish new rules for trade in agriculture, services, and intellectual property.

Security Ties

Since 1952 when the U.S.-Japan peace treaty went into effect, Japan has become a valued U.S. ally and a staunch member of the Western community. The bilateral arrangements established under the 1960 Treaty of Mutual Cooperation and Security have been crucial to peace and stability in East Asia. That treaty, spelling out our security relationship with Japan, is the cornerstone of U.S. security policy in the Pacific.

Japan's 1947 constitution precludes the projection of force abroad or an assertive military role in international relations. But Japanese perceptions of its security requirements have been made acute by Soviet intransigence on territorial issues, by the relentless Soviet military buildup in the Pacific, and by Moscow's aggression in Afghanistan and its support for Vietnam's invasion of Cambodia. A consensus has emerged in Japan which supports steady improvements in Japan's self-defense capabilities and expanded bilateral defense cooperation with the United States.

Our defense cooperation with Japan has never been better. Japan hosts some 60,000 U.S. troops and supports 7th Fleet ship visits and homeporting, including the only U.S. aircraft carrier battle group based overseas. Japan contributes $2.5 billion annually in "host-nation" support for U.S. Forces Japan. At over $40,000 per U.S. troop, that is the most generous "host-nation" support arrangement we have anywhere in the world. U.S. bases and facilities in Japan enable us to maintain regional defense capabilities, thus serving both U.S. and mutual security interests. We maintain these bases because it is in our own self-interest, our own self-defense, to do so.

The United States and Japan engage in extensive joint planning and exercises. Japan is participating in President Reagan's Strategic Defense Initiative (SDI), and transfers of important military technology from Japan to the United States are on the rise.

Just as Japan's "host-nation" support of U.S. forces and U.S.-Japan defense cooperation have increased, so has Japan's own self-defense efforts. Japan has undertaken to defend its territorial homeland, skies, and sealanes out to 1,000 nautical miles, providing a credible deterrent to Soviet adventurism in Northeast Asia. This allows flexibility for U.S. forces in case of emergencies in the Southwest Pacific and Indian Oceans. None of our forces in Japan is tied to the direct defense of Japan. Their role is regional.

These defense roles are consistent with Japanese and American expectations. They are in keeping with the views of Japan's neighbors which still remain sensitive to past militarism. Japanese defense spending rose 5.4% a year in real terms over the last 10 years. For FY 1988, the Japanese defense budget is $30 billion, fifth largest in the world and second largest of any non-nuclear power.

Mutual Need and Common Values

A book on U.S.-Japan relations just published by the Council on Foreign Relations is titled *For Richer, For Poorer*, and I want to borrow the metaphor of marriage it uses to characterize the U.S.-Japan relationship. Despite the competitive frictions in our partnership, we can profit more together than apart.

In many of our industries most affected by Japanese competition, such as electronics or autos, calls for barriers or "tough action" on trade cause us to overlook quietly successful U.S.-Japanese joint operations. All the U.S. auto companies have cross-invested and cross-marketed with their Japanese competitors. Electronics giants such as IBM, Motorola, Texas Instruments, and others have joint ventures, wholly owned subsidiaries, or both in Japan. More and more, as interrelationships grow to maturity among U.S. and Japanese companies, consumers will benefit and trade will grow.

In Japan today, the younger generation, raised in relative affluence, seems to be shifting to greater consumerism. The Japanese Government can help this trend and help U.S. products by removing structural inefficiencies, such as those in agriculture and distribution, which limit sales of foreign products most.

In contrast, Japan-Soviet relations are not close. The Soviets, since World War II, have occupied and militarized four Japanese islands known as the Northern Territories. Japan joined world condemnation of the Soviet invasion of Afghanistan and the occupation of Cambodia by Moscow's clients in Hanoi. It has helped provide UN refugee relief for the victims of these cruel tragedies. Following the Toshiba Machine Company affair, the Japanese Government and Japanese firms have become increasingly wary of Soviet interest in high technology.

In a fundamental sense, our mutual security and the security our alliance with Japan provides other friends and allies in the Pacific is as strong as it has ever been. At its core, it is sustained by beliefs both partners cherish dearly. A common faith in democracy, human rights, and free enterprise has permitted two great nations to remain competitors and friends for over three decades.

It is interesting to note that in recent years, the level and frequency of the U.S.-Japan bilateral dialogue has changed dramatically. Starting with Gerald Ford, all our Presidents have visited Japan while in office. President Reagan did so in 1983 and again in 1986 for Tokyo [economic] summit. During former Foreign Minister Abe's 4-year tenure, he and Secretary Shultz met almost 30 times. Subcabinet level meetings seem to be in almost constant session; all signs of a strong relationship with a key ally.

Despite its own self-image, Japan is not, and never has been, a poor island nation without natural resources. Japan's vibrant culture and industrious people have insured its strength and prosperity. Its modern combination of great financial power, cutting-edge technology, and strong international companies makes Japan a force to be taken seriously. It can make Japan a force for peace and progress, much as the United States has been in the postwar era.

Japan's leadership realizes that it must take actions to preserve the free market trading system, if for no other reason than to keep from being isolated in an increasingly trade-conscious world. But we need Japan to do more and have urged Japan to assume a global political role commensurate with its status as a world economic superpower. The Japanese leadership has sought to do that in numerous ways that support our shared foreign policy goals.

Japan has contributed to decision-making on U.S. arms control initiatives, including the U.S.-U.S.S.R. agreement on intermediate-range nuclear forces. In the Persian Gulf, where the U.S. fleet is protecting U.S. flag ships sailing to Japan and elsewhere with energy cargoes, Japan has taken steps to increase aid flows to Oman and Jordan and to install a precise navigational aid system with a $10 million price tag for the benefit of commercial mariners from all nations.

In the Philippines, Japanese aid flows have increased enormously since the Aquino government took the stage, amounting to over $600 million in JFY 1987. Prime Minister Takeshita made his first overseas trip a visit to Manila for an Association of South East Asian Nations (ASEAN) conference last December.

In fact Japan is the world's second largest donor of foreign aid after the United States. Together we provide about 45% of all economic assistance to developing nations. It is in this area that we are at work to map out constructive, mutually reinforcing strategies to benefit nations in need of growth and nourishment. Japan is the leading donor of economic aid to China and provides Korea with economic assistance as well. Tokyo gives aid to Egypt, Turkey and Pakistan, nations of strategic importance to the West. In short Japan has taken significant steps to play a larger role in the field of aid, and this has greatly benefitted stability and development in areas of vital interest to us both.

Structural changes in its economy can provide an even more important opportunity for Japanese cooperation. If Japan can accelerate imports of low and middle technology products, particularly from the developing world, it can offer a new opportunity for global economic growth which has been provided by the United States in the past. There are signs that this is happening. Japanese firms are erecting new factories in ASEAN countries, the United States, and Europe, but they have yet to export homeward as U.S. multinationals have.

We must continue to consult on international security, trade, and investment issues and encourage Japan to expand and deepen its role in the global economic institutions: the United Nations, the World Bank, the International Monetary Fund, the General Agreement on Tariffs and Trade, the Organization for Economic Cooperation and Development, and the international development banks. Trade is only one of several economic imbalances facing the United States, Japan, and the rest of the world. The Third World debt crisis threatens the international banking system. There is a glut of agricultural production worldwide, much of it caused by too much government support and artificial incentives to produce.

Now is a time of change, fraught with opportunity. The dawn of the information age offers challenges that the free nations of the world are best posed to meet, and the United States best of all. The example of Japan's economic ascent under a democratic, free-market orientation has invigorated Asia. Around the world, the American example of democracy and free enterprise is imitated, from the Philippines to Korea to Central America. Economic and political reforms in China, Hungary, and even the Soviet Union demonstrate this is true even behind the Iron Curtain. There is a connection between freedom and economic progress. We can be proud of our example.

There are pages we can borrow from the guide to Japanese success. We need to reduce budget deficits, to increase productivity and competitiveness, and to make more vigorous efforts to export quality goods.

Japan looks to the United States and sees lessons for itself. Japan seeks to imitate our success in higher education. Japanese brood over why a Japanese scientist won a Nobel prize for research performed in the United States, not at home where laboratories are hierarchically organized. Japanese pundits now look at the U.S. experience for clues as their own multinationals adopt overseas manufacturing strategies to survive the rapid appreciation of the yen.

After all the changes and adjustments in recent years, our $4.5 trillion economy remains significantly larger than Japan's, at $2.7 trillion. Japan's prosperity is dependent more than ours on stable overseas energy supplies. High land prices, directly related to Japan's protection of arciculture, deny most Japanese what is taken for granted by middle-class Americans, the ability to own your own home. It is amazing to read that the total price for Japan's land is more than twice that of all the land in the United States, with our natural resources and greater size.

In the U.S.-Japan relationship, as in many others, simplistic reactions to trade imbalances and economic adjustments are wrong, even counterproductive. We see rising employment, excellent products, and new technologies emerging all around us. Despite the adjustments forced by Japanese competition on many of our important industries, the bottom line is that total employment growth in the United States has outpaced that of Europe and Japan in this decade. U.S. manufacturing has achieved greater productivity to meet international competition, so that today our exports are booming and the goods-producing sector of our economy provides 22% of gross national product, which is consistent with our historical average.

So it is within the context of our global economic, political, and security partnership that we must deal with the serious trade imbalance between the United States and Japan. Our relationship today is at once broader, more complicated, and less divisible than just a few years ago. In our own interest, we must conduct our relations with Japan in such a way as to maximize the benefit for the United States and for Japan. If we do, together we will surely benefit the world.

RETHINKING JAPAN[8]

It was one of those moments that, in retrospect, mark a turning point. At his confirmation hearing in the plush room of the Senate Foreign Relations Committee, Secretary of State-nominee James A. Baker III was startled by a question on an obscure topic: Hadn't the outgoing Reagan Administration failed to consider the implications of jointly producing a new generation of fighter plane with the Japanese? Wouldn't the Japanese take the technology and beat us at our own game? The ever-gracious Baker promised that he would reexamine the issue as soon as he got back to Foggy Bottom.

[8]Reprint of an article by Robert Neff and Paul Magnusson, *Business Week* staff-writers. Reprinted from August 7, 1989 issue of *Business Week* by special permission. Copyright © 1989 by McGraw-Hill, Inc.

Four months later, a bruising battle within the Bush Cabinet was over, and the landscape of U.S.-Japan relations seemed forever changed. For the first time, policymakers treated America's economic strength as a national-security issue: Washington extracted from Tokyo a guarantee on how much of the FSX fighter business the U.S. would get, how much U.S. technology would be shared, and what new technology would flow back.

In doing so, the White House was openly acknowledging something that was already an article of faith on Wall Street and in Silicon Valley: Washington's tolerant and paternalistic policy toward Tokyo no longer reflected the relationship between the two economic giants. Even more important, many in the U.S. had come to question whether they had ever really understood Japan.

No less than a fundamental rethinking of Japan is now under way at the highest levels of U.S. government, business, and academia. The standard rules of the free market, according to the new school, simply don't work with Japan. The country is not evolving into a more open economy, say the adherents of the new thinking, but is driven by economic conquest and must be treated with different rules. "The deterioration of perception toward Japan is very obvious," says Yukio Okamoto, an official in Japan's Foreign Ministry.

Some people call the new thinking "revisionism," departing as it does from the orthodox view that Japan will eventually become a U.S.-style consumer-driven society. Revisionists believe Japan's power brokers have no such goals, are interested primarily in making Japan economically dominant in the world, and will only open up to trade partners when pushed to the wall. U.S. companies have discovered, says William T. Archey, a vice-president at the U.S. Chamber of Commerce, that "it doesn't matter how good you are, how hard-working, how much you look at the long term, or how much you spend on R&D. A Japanese decision to buy your product is not going to be based on the market principles we're familiar with."

The revisionists are out to prove that their detailed criticisms cannot be dismissed as those of Japan-bashers. Extensive research, years of living in Japan, and the trials of gridlocked trade talks all are used to depict how different Japan's political and economic institutions are from America's. "The idea that this is anti-Japanese is wrong," says Ivan Hall, a visiting professor of history at Keio University in Tokyo. "You can be critical of Germany and other countries without being branded as a basher."

Quick Jabs

The new thinkers come from a wide spectrum, including journalists, academics, Bush Cabinet members, and CEOs. Among the most prominent are U.S. political scientist Chalmers Johnson, Dutch journalist and author Karel van Wolferen, former trade official Clyde V. Prestowitz, and Commerce Secretary Robert A. Mosbacher.

A key element of revisionism is its rejection of conventional open-trade prescriptions. Instead, revisionists would seek guaranteed market shares or measurable results in Japan for American products that are globally competitive, such as supercomputers, semiconductors, and plywood. They would demand reciprocity in such highly protected sectors as banking, construction, and insurance. The penalty for not complying would be swift retaliation, cutting Japanese imports to the U.S. They would also expand the concept of "voluntary" export restrictions, which now exist for such Japanese exports as cars and steel.

Many revisionists also want Japan to untangle its complex distribution system and reform its antiquated land-use policies, which by protecting farmers discourage homebuilding. They want Japan to abandon its purchasing and easy-lending policies among members of the same industrial group. Though far from an ironclad rule, group loyalty counts. Visit a Mitsubishi Estate–owned building, and the elevators will probably be made by Mitsubishi Electric. Go out with Sumitomo Bank executives, and they'll choose restaurants serving beer from Asahi, a Sumitomo-group company that the bank helped turn around. This mentality makes Japan's market harder to crack than most.

Revisionists talk about a new industrial policy in America in which the government would encourage research and development cooperation and set up agencies to direct international trade and industry. The planned U.S. consortia to develop high-definition television and memory chips are fruits of such strategy. "Until now, the U.S. has treated the Japan question in a piece-meal, pell-mell fashion," says Kenneth S. Courtis, senior economist at Deutsche Bank Group in Tokyo. "The 1990s will see an integrated Japan policy incorporating trade, defense, aid, and technology."

The revisionist movement arrives at a key juncture. Just as the Soviet Union appears less threatening, more Americans are coming to view Japan as a national-security problem. Moreover, many believe that America is losing to Japan because of unfair trade practices, not just bad management and poor-quality products. As demonstrated in a mid-July Business Week/Harris Poll, almost 70% of the American adults surveyed termed the trade deficit with Japan a "very serious" problem. By a stunning 3-1 margin, the respondents named Japan's economic challenge as a greater threat to America's future than the Soviet military. And 68%, compared with 54% in a 1985 poll, said Japan is imposing unfair import barriers.

New Specter

The new mood in America presents U.S. policymakers with a troubling dilemma. Many U.S.-Japanese ties are vital. But the growing economic friction threatens the entire relationship. Mike Mansfield, former ambassador to Japan, liked to say that the U.S. and Japan have "the most important bilateral relationship in the world, bar none." In many ways, that is true. Americans depend on Japan for semiconductors, machine tools, and scores of favorite consumer goods. Japan's dollars make it easier to fund the national debt—and keep Americans consuming.

The Japanese in turn look to the U.S. as their largest market and strategic defender. The two countries' military partnership is crucial to the Pacific's defense and stability, and the two nations probably hold out the best hope for resolving the Third World debt crisis.

But after years of trying, the U.S. and Japan aren't getting things right when it comes to commerce. The $52 billion trade imbalance is barely down from when the dollar was strong, while over the same time, the U.S. trade deficit with Europe has halved. Aggressive Japanese investment in the U.S. is arousing alarm, and T. Boone Pickens Jr. is pointing out an embarrassing truth: It's far harder for Americans to buy big stakes in Japanese companies than vice versa.

At the same time, there seems to be a change in attitude in Japan, too. Many Japanese feel that after long years of sacrifice and hardship, they are ready to emerge onto center stage. Their per capita income has surpassed America's. Their GNP is larger than the Soviet Union's and is now 60% of America's. Many Japanese are scornful of complaints about their economy from a nation they believe to be a declining empire, and some are openly contemptuous of the U.S.

Yet Japan has serious problems, too. While business is booming, its political system is in crisis. On July 23, voters angry with multiple scandals in the ruling Liberal Democratic Party and a 3% consumption tax dealt the LDP a crushing blow in elections for the Diet's House of Councillors. Prime Minister Sousuke Uno said he would resign, but with no clear successor in sight, Japan's ruling party is in such disarray that its foreign policy may be unguided for many months. And since the strengthened opposition parties tend to be more protectionist, the U.S. will have to tread more carefully than ever to avoid a backlash.

Political turmoil at home is distracting most Japanese from the critics in America, if they were ever listening. And most of those who do listen downplay the significance of the new thinking. Some argue it is just protectionism and anti-Japanese bias in a more intellectually respectable form. Others say such views come from an outdated analysis of Japan, a country that is now changing rapidly in the direction Americans want.

Kazuo Nukazawa, managing director of Japan's powerful Federation of Economic Organizations, calls it "charlatan economics." Hidetoshi Ukawa, ambassador for International Economic Affairs, sees revisionism as "the U.S. wanting Japan to do all the changing without the U.S. doing its share" to correct its problems. But Hideo Ishihara, a managing director at the Industrial Bank of Japan Ltd., sees something more fundamental, even dangerous. "They're trying to force us to change things intrinsic to our values. This is probably the worst situation we've ever had. We are truly worried," he says.

U.S. trade policy styled after the revisionists' agenda could spell trouble for the General Agreement on Tariffs & Trade. Although much world trade is not truly free, GATT has long held out an ideal to strive for. Now, if the world's two largest trading nations deal with each other mainly outside GATT, its already weakened framework could come tumbling down.

Even if such a scenario is just a trade official's worst nightmare, "we definitely need to start looking at Japan as something besides a free-market economy," says Michael J. Farren, Commerce Under Secretary for international trade and a staunch revisionist. In achieving its postwar economic miracle, Japan put producers first and foremost. That meant protecting business, discouraging competition, and directing resources and economic spoils to the corporate sector so it could conquer world markets. Today, trade is viewed through the prism of national development and security, not consumer welfare.

It's not a question of right or wrong, fair or unfair, say most revisionists. Rather, it's a matter of fundamental divergence in economic and social structure and philosophy. Differences include the definitions of "open" and "fair," what constitutes an acceptable level of government intervention in commerce, and what's permissible or not. R&D consortia, cartels, and fixed pricing, for example, have long been common in Japan but rarely tolerated in the U.S. While the U.S. allows foreigners to make industrial investments virtually at will, Japan requires them to get a permit.

Japanese society has accepted things foreign—most of its laws and institutions are adaptations from the West. But a powerful elite directed the process in an orderly, deliberate fashion. Without official sanction, newcomers and new practices are seen as threatening the predictability and consensus necessary for harmony in a densely populated island nation. "Their barriers are much more sophisticated and subtle," says Commerce Secretary Mosbacher.

Perpetuating these values and elites is an educational system epitomized by Tokyo University's law department, the wellspring of virtually all top bureaucrats, most leading politicians, and many top executives in Japan. If there is a power center in the country, it is this school and its extensive network of alumni. The highly managed economy is its handiwork.

Japan's Finance Ministry, for example, allows only one kind of insurance policy at one price. In banking, rules to protect small financial institutions stymie the big banks. That means that a foreign bank like Citicorp, limited to one or two new branches a year, can never hope to compete with local banks. Foreign airlines are discouraged from boosting market share with discount prices. And despite a much-vaunted accord last year to open Japan's construction business, bid-rigging still flourishes at the expense of non-Japanese contractors. With little consumer consciousness and ingrained respect for authority, few Japanese complain.

"They really are a mercantilistic society," says former Deputy U.S. Trade Representative Michael B. Smith, now a trade consultant, referring to Japan's single-minded devotion to industrial supremacy. "I don't fault them for that. I do fault them for professing they are something else." Maureen Smith, Commerce Deputy Assistant Secretary for Japan and an eighty-year veteran of trade talks with Tokyo, says she has come to realize that the entire concept of free trade is disconcerting to the Japanese and antithetical to their sense of order. "They explain that competition would cause confusion in the market."

Turf Wars

Arrayed against this "confusion" are the government's powerful ministries such as Finance, International Trade & Industry, Transportation, and Posts & Telecommunications. So eager are these ministries to protect their turf that they sometimes block politicians. Despite the LDP government's assurances that Japan's mobile-phone market was open, for example, the Postal Ministry last spring devised regulations effectively closing the door. The LDP had to use all its political muscle to get the Ministry to yield. "There's not enough political control anywhere to affect basic changes in priority," concludes author van Wolferen. "The Americans have to do it for them."

A growing number of Bush Cabinet members seem prepared to attempt just that. In an annual trade study published in April, U.S. officials listed barriers to 33 products in Japan, more than were catalogued for any other country. Under the Super 301 provisions of the Omnibus Trade & Competitiveness Act of 1988, the Administration in May categorized Japan as a "priority" unfair trader in the areas of supercomputers, satellites, and forest products. Only India and Brazil were also named. Now, the U.S. has persuaded Japan to start talking about structural impediments to trade.

Before the Bush conversion, Congress was the focal point of efforts to rethink America's relationship with Japan. As early as 1984, Congress introduced the concept of reciprocity into legislation. President Reagan signed the 1988 Omnibus Act only reluctantly.

But the Bush Administration is picking up the ball as growing numbers of hard-liners, many of them Reagan-era holdovers who have learned tough lessons at the negotiating tables, assume important policymaking positions. Revisionists count among their fellow travelers such heavyweights as Mosbacher, Baker, and U.S. Trade Representative Carla A. Hills. Like-minded officials, such as Farren, Deputy U.S. Trade Representative S. Linn Williams, Under Secretary of State Richard T. McCormick, and Treasury Secretary David Mulford now populate dozens of key sub-Cabinet posts. Some observers put new Ambassador Michael H. Armacost in the same category.

Congress is still in there slugging, too. Always a hotbed of protectionist fervor, it is discovering that the revisionist school offers a respectable alternative to smashing Toshiba boom boxes on the steps of the Capitol. In addition, to Democratic leadership of both houses is increasingly populated by trade hawks. House Majority Leader Richard A. Gephardt (D-Mo.), who ran a faltering Presidential primary campaign on Japan and the trade deficit, is now pursuing the issue with more sophistication: He's even studying Japanese. Senator Lloyd Bentsen (D-Tex.), chairman of the powerful Senate Finance Committee, which has jurisdiction over trade matters, is a trade hawk of long standing. Add to that mix Senator John Heinz (R-Pa.), an advocate of results-oriented trade, Senator John C. Danforth (R-Mo.), and practically the entire Finance Committee membership.

The shift in thinking extends beyond Washington. In February, a blue-ribbon business-labor group, the Advisory Committee for Trade Policy & Negotiations, issued a pithy, widely noted report that jumped on the revisionist bandwagon, calling for tough results-oriented trade negotiations. "It's a landmark. Those are mainstream, Establishment business people," says Commerce's Smith. Among the high-powered executives in the business group are James D. Robinson III, chairman of American Express Co., and James R. Houghton, CEO of Corning Inc.

More important, there's growing popular support for a harder line on Japan. In many cases, large-scale Japanese investments in the U.S. haven't created the benefits many expected. Voters in Flat Rock, Mich., threw out their mayor for giving a 14-year tax holiday to Mazda Motor Corp. Kentucky's $150 million incentive package for a Toyota Motor Corp. plant helped former Governor Martha Layne Collins lose office. Workers at Nissan Motor Co.'s plant in Smyrna, Tenn., are locked in a bitter drive for a union. The view that integrating Japan into the U.S. economy is unquestionably good has hit some rough water.

As would any revisionist movement, this one has plenty of detractors. "The notion that Japan operates according to different rules is such garbage that it should be dismissed out of hand," says James C. Abegglen, a savvy management adviser to U.S. and Japanese companies in Tokyo. Others say the new thinking reflects resentment that America is no longer king of the mountain. Some even call it "Yellow Peril Revisited."

Open Question

Trade Representative Hills, too, while part of the new get-tough school, is wary of some of the prescriptions favored by congressional revisionists. She is opposed to demanding a percentage share of Japan's market but favors pressure for imports that seem to sell well other countries yet can't find many buyers in Japan. "Those who believe in managed trade to secure a percentage of a market are selling us short, demanding that we make do with what we can get," Hills says. She emphasizes reducing the federal budget deficit as a way of reducing spending for imports and raising U.S. savings.

Indeed, revisionism is still locked in a struggle with more conventional thinking. The State and Defense departments are warring with the Commerce Dept., insisting nothing be allowed to jeopardize the strategic relationship with Japan. How extensively the new thinking will affect policy, and in what form, is still an open question.

But these are good reasons to think revisionism will endure and even prosper. David Hale, chief economist at Kemper Financial Services, predicts that a swing to a more activist agenda is likely for the 1990s. After a decade of laissez-faire policies, America's infrastructure, education, relative productivity, and quality of life have declined. Congress, alarmed at the balance-of-payments crisis, has pushed itself permanently into international economic policymaking.

In fact, pressures are likely to intensify. Japanese industry is spending heavily to produce more goods for world markets, with capital investment in Japan topping that of the U.S. for the first time last year. Japanese investment in U.S. plants is also proceeding apace, pulling in massive imports of Japanese capital goods with it. As the American auto market slumps, Japanese carmakers, obsessed with market share, are expanding their Stateside dealer networks.

Still, the Japanese can claim to be making some progress toward mollifying the U.S. Their import of manufactured goods will probably exceed $100 billion this year, up from $59.6 billion in 1987. And Japan's GNP growth is currently coming entirely from domestic demand. "Things are changing rapidly in Japan," former Foreign Minister Saburo Okita wrote in *Japan Times* recently. "I wonder if the current problems are rooted in Japanese peculiarities or in the fact that our two countries are at different stages of development."

If revisionism is here to stay, both sides must somehow bridge the economic gulf without destroying the broader partnership. "Don't assume that Japan isn't going to lash out," warns Yoshi Tsurumi, professor of international business at Baruch College in New York. "Many Japanese will say, 'Let's say no to the U.S.'" The revisionists argue that's mostly rhetoric and at any rate, the U.S. can no longer afford to back down. In Tokyo, they call the new mood *tsumetai kaze*—a cold wind. The challenge for both countries now is to keep it from becoming a storm.

THE COMING U.S.-JAPAN CRISIS[9]

Television viewers in Japan saw an extraordinary news broadcast on the morning of July 2, 1987: nine members of the U.S. Congress were smashing a small Toshiba radio with sledgehammers at a press conference on Capitol Hill. The congressmen were expressing their anger at the Toshiba Machine Company of Japan, which had violated regulations of COCOM, the Coordinating Committee of multilateral export controls, by selling eight computer-guided multiaxis milling machines to the Soviet Union. The equipment permitted the Soviets to mass-produce a more silent propeller for their submarines and thus avoid detection by many of the current U.S. methods. One Pentagon official estimated that it would cost the United States some $30 billion to re-

[9]Reprint of an article by George R. Packard, Dean of the School of Advanced International Studies of the Johns Hopkins University in Washington, D.C., and Director of its Edwin O. Reischauer Center for East Asian Studies. Reprinted by permission of *Foreign Affairs*, Winter 1988. Copyright © 1987 by the Council on Foreign Relations, Inc.

gain the technological superiority lost in the illegal sale. The sledgehammer scene, which was largely ignored by the American media, was shown over and over again in Japan, to the point where it now lodges uneasily in the collective national consciousness.

The anger of the congressmen was understandable. From the facts then available (and neither the Japanese government nor Toshiba Corporation, parent of the Toshiba Machine Company, has denied them), the security breach was considerable, and possibly irreparable. As seen from Capitol Hill, an ungrateful Japan, still spending only about one percent of its GNP for defense, still protected by American forces and a U.S. defense budget which consumes about six percent of GNP, was aiding a potential adversary for profit.

But the event triggered far more complex emotions on both sides, and reflected growing mutual frustrations. For many American leaders, Japan was already guilty of running up a huge trade surplus through questionable tactics while keeping its own market largely closed to American products. Spectacular advances by Japanese engineers in a variety of high technology fields raised the specter of losses in one after another American industry, following the fate of such industries as steel, television, automobiles, machine tools and, most recently, certain kinds of semiconductors.

On the other hand, Japanese reactions included a mixture of shock, anger and embarrassment. A number of industry leaders expressed the view that the entire Japanese nation should not be held responsible for the sins of one private corporation. They noted that no Norwegian products had been smashed, even though a Norwegian state-controlled enterprise, Kongsberg Vaapenfabrikk, had been judged equally guilty of violating the COCOM regulations. (In October 1987 the Norwegian government disclosed that Kongsberg had shipped more than 140 banned computers to the Soviet Union and had cooperated with companies based in France, Italy and West Germany to ship other high-tech equipment to the Russians during the past ten years. Still no Norwegian products were smashed on Capitol Hill.) Many Japanese believed the Americans were venting their frustration over their own inability to restore competitiveness and balance the federal budget. A variety of Japanese viewers found the televised spectacle to be unworthy of elected officials, and some suspected a U.S. conspiracy to hold back Japan's progress in high technology.

As if to fulfill Japan's suspicions, and vent its own wrath, the Senate approved by an overwhelming majority in late June a provision in the omnibus trade bill demanding compensation and banning Toshiba imports for two to five years. This action triggered an immediate reaction from American distributors of Toshiba products as well as a number of leading U.S. corporations, who argued that the ban could cause grave economic damage to the dozens of American companies which depend on Toshiba parts. It seemed clear by late autumn that the ban would be significantly watered down or removed altogether before the trade bill became law. But the emotions rubbed raw by the episode lingered on. Dealing with this crisis of confidence will be an immense challenge for Japan's newly chosen prime minister, Noboru Takeshita.

II

There is a volatility and an emotional quality to Japanese-American relations that is unique. At the turn of the century the Japanese were viewed sentimentally as America's favored protégés, a diligent, clean but backward island people who eagerly sought our scientific, technical and even moral insights. But almost overnight, after Japan sank the Russian fleet in 1905, it came to be regarded as part of the "yellow peril"—a threat to our new empire in the Pacific, a scheming predator with designs even on Mexico. In 1906 the San Francisco Board of Education excluded Japanese children from its regular schools, and Congress soon passed laws (aimed especially at Japanese) barring Orientals from immigrating to the United States. Racial hatred was never far from the surface along the long, dreary road to Pearl Harbor. It exploded with a vengeance in World War II.

From the postwar period to the early 1970s, Japanese were content once again to accept vast amounts of American culture, democracy and economic tutelage. Americans were pleased to view Japan once again as an eager, docile and nonthreatening ally in the Pacific.

Since the 1970s we have seen a gradual decline of trust, at least at the government level. As Japanese exports have poured into American markets, Japanese corporations have been accused

Japan and the U.S.

of conducting "adversarial trade," ta~~~~
try after another for destruction. For th~~~~
have become privately critical of American~~~~
traordinary friendship between President Ro~~~~
Prime Minister Yasuhiro Nakasone tended to obs~~~~
undercurrents of hostility within the higher levels of g~~~~
and the private sectors on both sides.

Despite the hostility at this leadership level, at the grass ~~~~
Japanese and Americans continue to be fascinated with each ot~~~~
er. As emotions have waxed and waned over the years, neither
trade wars nor a shooting war have dampened the mutual enthusiasm for learning from each other at the grass roots. Japanese
admire American creativity, optimism, openness, egalitarianism,
self-confidence and enthusiasm for free enterprise. Americans
are impressed with Japan's sense of history, aesthetics, reserve
and, most recently, its managerial, scientific and technological
genius, and its growing wealth.

There is, however, a continuing penchant among leaders on
both sides of the Pacific to misunderstand and usually to underes-
timate each other. Woodrow Wilson dismissed Japanese requests
for a racial equality clause in the Covenant of the League of Nations, though he had studied at Johns Hopkins University with In-
azo Nitobe, Japan's great internationalist who later served as
deputy secretary of the League of Nations from 1919 to 1926.
Franklin D. Roosevelt turned down Prime Minister Fumimaro
Konoye's request for a meeting on the eve of World War II on
the advice of the U.S. ambassador, Joseph Grew, who spent ten
years in Tokyo without bothering to learn the Japanese language
or to cultivate Japan's real leaders.

Japan's military leaders attacked Pearl Harbor in the conviction that Americans were too weak and preoccupied in Europe
to fight back. Then in 1954 John Foster Dulles told a congressional committee that Japan lacked the skills to export much of
anything to the United States, but might find a few markets in
Southeast Asia. As for Japan, although Prime Minister Nakasone
stood as an exception, most Japanese postwar government and
business leaders have preferred to entrust direct contacts with
American counterparts to a trained corps of "barbarian
handlers."

In sum, only a tiny and fragile network of personal friendships cushions the shock of conflicting interests in the manner,

can leaders to settle

y at work. Japan, having
g creditor nation of the
chnology and supplied an
manufactured goods. The
eathtaking trade surplus of
g March 31, 1987. Mean-
mbed to an unprecedented
llion was with Japan.

The U.   legislation its highest priority
and aimed several p.   asures squarely at Japan. The
2,000-plus pages of the trade   ontained an enormous variety
of measures aimed at protecting the domestic market and forcing
open markets abroad. Some provisions sought to limit investment
by other nations whose own economies were closed to U.S. investment. Reciprocity and "a level playing field" were the central
themes. Congressman Richard Gephardt (D-Mo.) anchored his
presidential ambitions to an amendment aimed at forcing down
Japan's trade surplus and limiting presidential discretion to negotiate. An appreciation of the yen versus the dollar by more than
60 percent since the September 1985 Plaza Agreement on monetary exchange rates had failed to stem the rising tide of Japanese
exports.

In March of this year Fujitsu Ltd. was discouraged from ac-
quiring the Fairchild Semiconductor Corporation on competitive
and national security grounds, although Fairchild was already in
the hands of the French-owned company Schlumberger Ltd. In
April President Reagan ordered the first trade sanctions against
Japan since World War II—a 100-percent tariff against some
$300 million worth of Japanese exports containing chips—in re-
taliation for Japan's alleged violation of a 1986 semiconductor
agreement.

Even before the revelation of Toshiba Machine Company's il-
licit sales to the Soviet Union, the media on both sides became
strident, even belligerent. Japanese charged that the American
budget deficit lay at the heart of the problem. Why couldn't the
president and Congress balance the budget and restore American

industrial competitiveness instead of making scapegoats of the Japanese? The American media, while generally opposing protectionism, carried charges by U.S. business and government leaders that the Japanese were engaging in unfair trade practices, targeting U.S. industries for annihilation, dumping products in an open American market and closing the Japanese market to outsiders through a variety of non-tariff barriers. "Japan-bashing" took on a new kind of respectability.

Two widely quoted articles captured the essence of American grievances. The late Theodore White, in an emotional *New York Times Magazine* article in July 1985, argued that a relentless Japanese economic juggernaut aimed at deindustrializing America was seeking to win the "War of the Pacific" through unfair economic tactics, having lost the opening battle of conventional military forces.

More recently, Karel G. van Wolferen, a Dutch journalist, contended in an article in *Foreign Affairs* that the Japanese do not accept free enterprise and free trade as it is understood in the West, that the Japanese business-government alliance is out to "systematically undermine Western industries" through "adversarial trade," and that there is no political or decision-making center in Tokyo capable of shifting gears.

Media criticism led to shifts in public opinion polls. A *New York Times*/CBS–Tokyo Broadcasting System survey taken in May 1987 showed that 55 percent of those Japanese polled viewed Japan-U.S. relations as "unfriendly," up dramatically from less than one third who held that view a year earlier. And a *Washington Post*/ABC poll taken the same month showed that 63 percent of Americans supported higher trade barriers, as against 49 percent in 1985. (Still, 77 percent of Americans viewed relations with Japan as "friendly.") Finally, and astoundingly, an *Asahi Shimbun* poll of April 1987 showed that the People's Republic of China was now the favorite foreign nation of the Japanese people, bumping the United States into second place for the first time since the Vietnam War days. Ironically, this fondness did not seem reciprocal; Chinese criticisms of Japan increased sharply in 1987.

What was new in all this was the suspicion both in Washington and Tokyo that the other nation was pursuing divergent goals for the first time since World War II. High-level officials in Washington have come to wonder whether Japan would again become a

military rival in the Pacific. Officials in Tokyo worried that the
West was once again ganging up on Japan—a worry that goes
back at least as far as the Triple Intervention of 1897, when
France, Russia and Germany pressured Japan into giving up a
piece of Chinese territory it had won in the Sino-Japanese War
of 1894–95.

IV

Underlying the harsh rhetoric of the trade dispute is the often forgotten reality that the two nations are more tightly intertwined economically and militarily than ever before.

Export industries have led Japan's economic growth in the
past decade. Japan depends on the American market to absorb
nearly 40 percent of its exports, and this dependence will not
change soon. Conversely, during the past five years of massive
U.S. budget deficits, the flow of Japanese capital into U.S. Treasury bonds and corporate securities has kept U.S. interest rates
low and sustained an economic recovery. The cumulative impact
of Japanese investment in the United States has given Japan a
huge stake in sustaining the value of its dollar investments and
avoiding a serious U.S. recession that would decrease that value.
In short, the Japanese need a healthy American economy as much
as Americans do, and most Japanese government and industry
leaders are quick to recognize this fact both publicly and privately.

A commission chaired by the former governor of the Bank of
Japan, Haruo Maekawa, offered a blueprint for structural reform
of the Japanese economy that recognized this growing interdependence. The Maekawa report, issued in April 1986 and elaborated upon in April 1987, called for an urgent effort to stimulate
domestic demand, reduce dependence on exports, cope with out-
rageously high land prices, improve housing, shorten working
hours, spur competition in the distribution of rice, and lower
trade barriers to other agricultural products—all within two to
three years. The report recommended that taxes be reduced, imports of manufactured goods increased, foreign investment in Japan encouraged, remaining trade barriers reduced, and domestic
capital markets liberalized. The government of Japan was urged
to play a greater role in resolving the Third World debt crisis,
furnish more overseas development assistance and increase imports from the less developed countries.

While skeptics inside and outside Japan tended to dismiss the Maekawa report as more of the same old empty promises, the truth was that important elements of Japan's ruling elite had recognized that Japan's mercantilist policies could not continue without disrupting the entire system of free trade on which Japan's prosperity depends. Whether these elements would ultimately prevail hung in the balance in the autumn of 1987. Clearly Japan has entered a great national debate. So far, at least, a general consensus is moving toward acceptance of the Maekawa recommendations. The greatest danger is that a new surge of nationalism, stimulated by Japan-bashing from abroad, could block the forces of healthy change.

Opening Japan's markets will cause more than the usual amount of pain. The obvious place to begin is in the agricultural sector. Japan has protected its inefficient farmers to the point where Japanese consumers must pay five or six times the world price for rice and three or four times the American price for beef. The system perpetuates itself, first, because successive Liberal Democratic Party (LDP) governments have relied on the farm vote and still do—although to a lesser extent now than in earlier years. Second, Japanese have revered for centuries the ideal of farming and the culture of rice. Even today most urban Japanese maintain close ties with relatives in some remote rural area, and many formal ceremonies involve rice wine (sake), rice paper, rice straw or baskets. Finally, the outside world has always seemed alien, hostile or even threatening, which has created an age-old disposition among Japanese to avoid dependence on any foreign power for such basics as food.

A number of leading opinion-makers in Japan, such as commentator and author Kenichi Omae, have recently come forward with land reform plans aimed at turning rice paddies into housing developments. Farmers would lose their low-property-tax status and would be forced from the cultivation of fields in the urban and suburban areas. Land prices, which have skyrocketed in the past several years, would ease downward. Credit would flow to home-builders and buyers, who would quickly seize the chance to escape from their cramped apartments. The resulting boom in construction, home appliance sales, suburban infrastructure and leisure activities could fuel a new era of growth that would be less dependent on exports and might even increase imports.

All of this will probably come to pass, but the process will be slow and painful, and the results will not greatly ameliorate U.S.-Japan trade relations within the next five years, when the danger of combustion is the greatest. In any event, it is certain that Japan will never entirely abandon its farming. Imports of California rice will be grudging and incremental.

V

Despite trade frictions the U.S.-Japan military relationship is working better than at any time since the revised Treaty of Mutual Cooperation and Security took effect in 1960. Japan still views the Soviet threat more calmly than the United States, but it has taken substantial steps to build up its defensive capabilities and to integrate its forces with those of the United States.

There are still critics in Congress and the Pentagon who argue that Japan is not doing its fair share. The Nakasone cabinet breached the self-imposed one-percent-of-GNP limit on defense spending set ten years earlier by another conservative cabinet (but not by much; in the current budget year defense spending will amount to 1.004 percent of GNP). This will presumably remove some of the political and psychological restraints against even greater defense spending. But Japanese leaders were shocked by harsh criticism from China over this step, and they continue to face strong domestic opposition to a more rapid military buildup. Thus it seems clear that American advocates of faster Japanese rearmament will be disappointed for some years to come.

An astonishing episode, however, may give these same critics second thoughts about the wisdom of pushing the Japanese defense capabilities. Having urged the Japanese since 1953 to ignore Article IX of their own constitution, which prohibits the maintenance of offensive war-waging potential, the Pentagon was greatly disturbed to learn that the Japanese in early 1987 were considering a plan to design and build their own jet fighter, the FSX, for the 1990s. This sent shockwaves through the American aerospace industry, which correctly viewed the plan as an effort by Japan to build up a more competitive aircraft industry. It also signaled the coming of age of a significant new military-industrial complex in Japan that would exert a great deal of clout over domestic and foreign policy in the years ahead.

From the time of Secretary of Defense Caspar Weinberger's visit to Tokyo in June 1987 until last October, the issue was argued behind the scenes among Japanese politicians and business leaders. None of them doubted Japan's ability to make a better fighter plane than any that could be produced in American industry, though the unit cost might be higher. All of them agreed on the economic and political benefits of developing Japan's independent aerospace industry. And most of them viewed the issue as one of national pride: Japan should move forward in every area of high technology, regardless of American displeasure. Weren't the Americans again trying to hold down Japanese technological progress on all fronts?

It took the Toshiba incident and the pending American trade legislation to induce Prime Minister Nakasone and Defense Agency Minister Yuko Kurihara to stand up to the forces of "techno-nationalism" in Tokyo. After much agonizing and quiet pressure from Washington, Minister Kurihara announced on October 2, 1987, that Japan would use either the General Dynamics Corporation's F-16 or the McDonnell Douglas Corporation's F-15 as the basic model, with some modifications, for 100 aircraft to be used in the 1990s. While the plane will be built largely in Japan, the licensing agreement will ensure that at least $1 billion and several thousand jobs come to the United States. Later in October Japan appeared to have chosen to produce 130 F-16 aircraft under license from General Dynamics.

It was significant that Senator John Danforth (R-Mo.), a leading advocate of tougher trade measures against Japan, also hails from the state which is home to both McDonnell Douglas and General Dynamics. The Japanese understood, correctly, that a decision to go it alone would have produced a firestorm on Capitol Hill. They would have been charged with exacerbating the U.S. trade deficit. The political and military alliance would have become hopelessly entangled with economic questions. The forces for Japan-bashing would have been strengthened, and the Toshiba sanctions would almost certainly have become law.

The whole Toshiba-FSX affair may in the end produce two perversely beneficial results. First, to ward off further sanctions against Toshiba, Defense Minister Kurihara also announced on October 2 a new research program intended to improve both nations' ability to detect submarines, as well as a Defense Agency plan to take other long-overdue steps to build up its antisubmarine warfare capabilities. Second, the episode may bring new caution to those who have been pushing Japan to do more rearming. It should now be clear to them that there are forces in Japan ready and willing to go much farther and faster down the road to an independent military force—with or without U.S. approval. Prime Minister Takeshita could be more responsive to their pressure.

With its massive economic strength, Japan should most certainly do more to defend the security arrangements from which it has benefited. By every lesson of history and common sense, however, its contribution should come in the form of development assistance to nations of critical importance in the strategic balance. The good news is that Japan has been moving steadily in this direction. The bad news is that the movement has always been too little and too late, and always in response to American pressure.

It is still true, nevertheless, that the U.S.-Japan security treaty is working better today than ever before. As further evidence of the growing military interdependence of the two nations, the Pentagon has requested, and since 1985 Japan has agreed to transfer, certain dual-use technologies—the first such transfer of Asian military technology to a Western power in recent memory. We can expect that Japan will develop new technologies which will be of interest to the United States, including those flowing from its participation in the Strategic Defense Initiative. Mr. Nakasone considerably broadened the interpretation of Article IX when he declared in September in the Diet that Japanese minesweepers could legally operate in the Persian Gulf.

VI

Despite these objective conditions—or perhaps to some extent *because* neither side can see a happy way out of depending on the other—the American-Japanese dialogue has become increasingly acrimonious. For Japanese leaders, America has become a clumsy ally—almost an embarrassment. The president and Congress seem unable to balance the budget. This, plus a general loss of competitiveness, has led to the huge American trade deficits and the dramatic stock market declines of October. American politicians once again became mired in a Watergate-like scandal in the Iran-contra affair. One after another candidate on the

Democratic side is wounded or eliminated by affairs that seem inscrutable. Meanwhile, Japan serves as scapegoat. "What is wrong with making good products?" an official protested privately last summer. "Nobody is forcing the American people to buy our goods."

As Japan's prosperity grows, albeit at a pace slower than in the 1970s, as its cities and rural areas flourish, Japanese leaders who visit the United States see its urban squalor, bankrupt farmers, shoddy transportation systems and its widespread problems of crime, drugs and racial animosity, and tend to believe that the United States is finished as a great power. Prime Minister Nakasone's remark of September 1986, that America's racial minorities tend to keep its educational level low, reflected a widely held but normally unstated view among Japanese leaders.

Japanese leaders look over their shoulders and see South Korea and other newly industrialized countries challenging them and forcing them into higher value-added advanced technology industries. For centuries Japanese leaders have felt vulnerable to external shocks, from tsunami and earthquakes to Commodore Matthew Perry's Black Ships and atomic weapons. They have devised various ways of coping with insecurity, including playing on their isolation and insularity and exalting the superiority of certain national characteristics.

As recently as in the 1930s and during World War II the Japanese people were told they were a divine race, descended from the Sun Goddess, possessed of a unique purity and virtue. It should not be forgotten that all of Japan's leaders who are over 55 today were formally educated to accept this myth, though most educated Japanese did not.

The national virtue currently being exalted is Japan's genius for high technology and its progress toward a new utopia—an Information Society. Japan will make its mark, assure itself of security and prosperity, and give vent to its special kind of nationalism by being first on the frontiers of science and technology. Yet everywhere they look, long shadows play upon the success of the Japanese. Protectionism threatens to close markets abroad. Warfare in the Persian Gulf threatens their oil supply, on which all else depends. And at home demands are growing that Japan's newly acquired wealth should be more widely shared among ordinary citizens. Former U.S. Ambassador to Japan Edwin O. Reischauer believes Japan has fostered "unhealthy economic growth." "Among the developed countries," he wrote to me recently, "Japan stands out as the worst example of poor housing, poor public facilities such as sewage disposal, hospitals, school buildings, parks, roads and space for amusements." Japan's leaders are coming belatedly to the realization that wrenching change lies ahead. A great national debate is raging beneath the surface, not about whether change will come, but rather about how and when it will come and how it will be managed.

Japanese opinion leaders and decision-makers are tending in this debate toward the old error of underestimating American vitality and resilience. If dependence on America hurts their national pride, they are also frustrated by the lack of attractive alternatives. To abandon the security treaty with the United States would require unacceptably high defense costs—and a crippling domestic struggle over whether to possess nuclear weapons. It might also result in a loss of U.S. market share and severe restrictions on future direct and indirect investments in the United States. There is a Soviet card to play, but Japanese leaders long ago weighed the advantages of joining in the development of Siberia, with its possibilities for investment, exports, access to raw materials and profits from joint enterprises, and concluded that partnership with the United States was safer, more profitable and more congenial in general than dealing with the Soviets, who have ever appeared threatening and untrustworthy.

The resulting paralysis will not come from any lack of central organs of government which can recognize what is good for Japan and bear ultimate responsibility for national decision-making, as Mr. van Wolferen suggested in his *Foreign Affairs* article. On the contrary, since World War II the Japanese have demonstrated in crises an extraordinary capacity to set a national course based on achievable goals and take whatever actions was required to follow it. Their decision to shift abruptly from encouraging population growth before the end of World War II to discouraging such growth at the end of the war was taken at the highest levels of government and propagated efficiently, resulting in an almost immediate decline in the birthrate.

Similarly, as shown in a recent Harvard Business School study, Japanese government and business leaders adopted a well-planned economic strategy in the 1950s aimed at raising Japan's standard of living to that of Europe and America through intensive and carefully staged employment of capital and technology. Japan entered into a revised security treaty with the United States in 1960 despite massive protests in the streets of Tokyo. In 1979–80, after the second oil shock, it joined with other Western nations to attempt to limit OPEC's power. After the Soviet invasion of Afghanistan in 1980, Japan, unlike most U.S. allies, joined in a boycott of the Moscow Olympics.

Decisions are made differently in Japan, through seemingly endless discussions, meetings, reports and exchanges ending in consensus. Yet this should not blind us to the fact that rational decisions have been made on the basis of both extraordinary vision and common sense and, further, that implementation can be extraordinarily rapid once consensus has been achieved. To contend, as Mr. van Wolferen does, that Japan "has no top" is to miss the point entirely. The "top" in an advanced democracy, whether Japan, the United States or Western Europe, is where you find it in any given political season.

Rather, the problem today is that Japan's foreign economic policy has been far too successful. Now it must change. Japan cannot continue to protect its home market while piling up record surpluses year after year. The current dilemma is that the internationalists such as Mr. Nakasone and Haruo Maekawa are attempting to convince a highly successful democracy that it must voluntarily change the very strategies that have led to unprecedented prosperity. What politician will have the courage to openly come out for policies that would ruin Japan's traditional farming communities, destroy leading exporters, allow foreign corporations to own a portion of its most technologically advanced industries, or let foreign banks influence interest rates? What business leader will stand up and say that Japan's current export-led consumption and spending spree must yield to slower growth? Merely to ask these questions is to point to the unlikelihood that change will come soon or easily.

On the other hand, few nations have managed wrenching change as well as Japan over the past century, and many signs suggest that the Japanese are once again girding themselves for a new era. The challenge facing both America and Japan is to manage the coming change without reviving an unhealthy Japanese nationalism that could destroy a mutually beneficial economic and security relationship. American diplomacy must exert steady, quiet pressure aimed at supporting Japan's internationalists and avoiding the kind of emotional bashing that strengthens the nationalists.

VII

If one examines closely the existing governmental agencies for managing the U.S.-Japan relationship, the situation appears nearly hopeless.

In Washington it is hard to discover a "Japan policy." There is no part of the executive branch whose mission it is to oversee all aspects of the relationship. The State and Defense Departments, which in the 1960s exerted dominant influence in creating political and military policies toward Japan, have seen their power eroded by new claims from Commerce, Treasury, Agriculture and the Office of the U.S. Trade Representative as economic issues have risen to the fore. Today a welter of intergovernmental working groups, task forces and coordinating bodies share bits of the action, but no one department or agency can be said to be in charge.

To this disarray one must add the growing power and interest of Congress or, more precisely, of individual members, committees and staff members concerned with particular aspects of the relationship, such as protecting an industry against Japanese imports or gaining access to the Japanese market for a constituent. To the mix must also be added an ever-increasing army of lobbyists and special interest groups, some representing Japanese interests and some working for American corporations. These lobbyists often turn out to be former officials from the very U.S. government agencies they are now trying to influence. It has even been charged by some congressional staff members that current U.S. government officials lean one way or another on issues in hopes of jumping subsequently to a lucrative lobbying position with one of the special interest groups.

None of this is particularly new to Washington nor unique to the U.S.-Japan relationship, but the result of all the tugging and pulling is that U.S. behavior toward Japan is eccentric, episodic and devoid of any long-term vision of where this important relationship should be headed and how it will get there. Japanese negotiators have learned to wait patiently until today's issue gives way to tomorrow's. They cannot be blamed for failing to understand or act upon American priorities, for no one can say at any moment what these priorities are.

One might argue that wiser leadership and better management could bring order from this chaos. Indeed it is possible to cite other relationships where sound policy and effective diplomacy have combined to advance the U.S. national interest in spectacular ways, such as in the Nixon-Kissinger reopening of relations with the People's Republic of China. In Washington's China policy, as in its Soviet policy, there is, for better or worse, a conceptual framework within which specific policies can be developed. Americans who specialize in Chinese or Soviet affairs generally have a voice in policy formulation. There is also a widely shared presumption that serious U.S. national interests are at stake.

None of this is true for Washington's Japan policy. No referee oversees the tug-of-war politics among competing agencies and interest groups. No one seems able to draw conclusions about the proper balance between Japan as a trusted ally in East Asia and Japan as a tough economic competitor. Japan specialists, with occasional exceptions, are not considered a vital part of the policymaking process, and are sometimes excluded entirely on the grounds that they may be too sympathetic toward Japan. The economic issues have become so complex in any case that no specialist can be expert in all matters ranging from soybeans to semiconductors. Yet our relations with Japan are at least as important as those with China and the Soviet Union.

The Japanese government, with fewer personnel in the relevant agencies and fewer bureaucrats in the decision-making process, is better equipped to negotiate complex issues and manage the relationship according to an overall strategy. The Finance Ministry, the Ministry of International Trade and Industry (MITI) and the Foreign Ministry all have well-trained and competent America specialists who tend to remain longer or return more often to the same issues, giving Tokyo a major advantage in international knowledge and expertise. It is doubtful that any politician—even a prime minister—could assert a special interest over the general national interest as defined by senior bureaucrats in these ministries.

Yet Tokyo will find it increasingly difficult to resolve economic issues with the United States for a different set of reasons. First, many senior bureaucrats are wedded to outdated policies under which Japan must forever concentrate on exporting manufactured goods, even though these exports produce a flood of protectionist measures in Japan's best overseas markets.

Second, to the extent that Liberal Democratic Party members are gradually entering into policymaking roles, evidence so far suggests they will represent single-interest groups in their constituencies rather than Japan's national interest, and that these interests overwhelmingly favor an untenable status quo. And Japan today lacks a cadre of *genro* (senior statesmen) who can successfully assert the national interest over various special interest groups.

Third, Prime Minister Takeshita, though equally committed to maintaining the U.S.-Japan partnership, is a far more cautious politician than Mr. Nakasone. The former finance minister's strength lies in his long experience in domestic political maneuvering. The fact that he leads the largest LDP faction in the Diet will encourage Americans to expect quick reforms in Japan. Barring some new "shock" to Japan's economy, however, it is likely that he will move so slowly in forming a consensus that American policymakers and politicians will find fresh cause for outrage.

Fourth, Japan is already challenging the United States with a major new drive toward creativity and leadership in advanced technology. This drive is neither sinister nor secret. MITI announced as long ago as 1980 its plan to create a series of 19 "Silicon Valleys"—to be known as "technopolises"—throughout 16 prefectures of Japan. This bold public-private initiative will bring together new, advanced-technology plants in industrial parks with universities and the needed infrastructure of airports, roads and recreational facilities. All of this is based on the premise that Japan has largely caught up with Western science and technology and that any new advances must come from the creative genius of the Japanese people themselves. The government is also considering ways to reform the Japanese education system from top to bottom to foster greater creativity.

Given Japan's record to date, it would be foolish to doubt that this strategy will result in spectacular advances and growing supremacy in a variety of fields such as industrial ceramics, lasers, semiconductors, biotechnology, solar energy, robotics, superconductors and possibly in space exploration. These advances, in turn, will be largely used in consumer products and will lead to *increasing* exports, rising "techno-nationalism," and deepening fears among Americans that we can no longer compete. Japanese bureaucrats and politicians will be sorely tempted to seek new avenues for national advancement. American officials will find it harder than ever to ward off self-defeating protectionist measures. The media will have a field day publishing the charges and countercharges of angry politicians. Public opinion in both nations could take an ugly turn. Traditional diplomacy will fail.

VIII

Trade issues are inherently boring or incomprehensible to most senior policymakers, who would much rather deal with grand strategy than beef or semiconductors. This situation allows the dialogue between the United States and Japan to be dominated by a cacaphony of those lawyers, lobbyists and businessmen who have a direct personal stake in the outcome of legislation that will never become known even to those Americans generally knowledgeable about international affairs. It is for this reason that traditional bureaucratic and diplomatic methods cannot solve our current crisis with Japan.

Instead of leaving economic problems to the politicians, bureaucrats, lobbyists and media on both sides, consideration should be given to the establishment of a permanent "Wisemen's Commission" of four or five experienced statesmen on each side. The idea is not new, but the current tensions give it a new urgency.

The commissioners would meet once a month and direct a permanent staff to get the facts and recommend fair solutions. Commissioners would include, but not be limited to, individuals with experience in Japanese-American affairs. They would represent a broad cross-section of each nation with representatives of the interests of business and labor, agriculture, science and technology, education and culture, and would include women and minorities. They would vote as individuals from the private sector rather than as government delegates. Unlike the previous two Wisemen's Commissions under Presidents Carter and Reagan, which had only short lifetimes of 18 months, the fact that this commission would be permanent could result in more follow-through and oversight. The two governments could, of course, ignore the commission's recommendations, but only at a cost. The media could be counted on to publicize those recommendations for dispute resolution that were deemed "fair" by respected private-sector individuals in each country.

The commissioners should have five-year renewable terms and a skilled permanent staff able to deal with language, cultural,

economic and technological problems. Let each government pay
up to half the expenses of the commission, with the private sector
paying the other half of each side. Let each government agree in
advance to accept the findings of the commission and, in specific
instances, let it mediate trade disputes. In this way issues could be
settled in an atmosphere which is free from emotional nationalism, where the facts are not in dispute, and in accordance with
the overriding interest of each nation in maintaining a cooperative relationship.

All kinds of objections would immediately arise: it will be hard
to find truly wise individuals who are acceptable to both sides;
other nations would view this as exclusive binationalism, a road-
block to multilateral freedom of trade. Politicians in both countries would cry out against allowing national decisions to come
under the influence of an international body. Bureaucrats would
correctly see this as a curb on their power and would fight tooth
and nail against it.

But wise and decisive leadership on each side could prevail.
A future U.S. president and Japanese prime minister could use
the Wisemen's Commission as a building block toward freer international trade. It could defuse protectionist sentiment and re-
lieve congressmen and Diet members of the burden of making
unpopular decisions. It could be an inclusive body, aimed at eventually bringing others such as Canada or the United Kingdom
into the arrangement.

The commission would recognize that the sum of all the special interest groups on each side of the Pacific is not equivalent
to the national interest of either country, that the special interest
groups may legitimately pursue their profits and loudly lobby
their legislatures, but that transcending goals must prevail. Har-
monious relations between the United States and Japan are, and
will be in the future, in the vital interests of both democracies.
Or, to put it the other way around, a breach leading to open hostility would undermine the entire balance-of-power system which
has brought, and continues to bring, stability and dramatic economic growth to East Asia in the postwar era. It would be irratio-
nal for each nation to risk such a course, but rationality has not
been our hallmark over the past century.

The commission could be charged with the task of developing
a plan for complete freedom of trade between the United States
and Japan by the end of the next decade, along the lines of the

free trade agreement reached by the United States and Canada in October 1987. It could save thousands of hours of bureaucratic bickering every day and allow leaders on both sides to work toward grander visions. They would address the basic insecurities and vulnerabilities of each nation and try to find long-range solutions to these questions. Obviously its work would ultimately require the approval of both governments through their normal processes. But the negotiations aimed at reaching intergovernmental accords could be conducted by the "wisemen" in an atmosphere free of emotion and lobbying by special interests, since the negotiators would have neither bureaucratic turf to defend nor an election to face every two years.

Both Japan and America entertain serious doubts about their national security over the long run. Japan worries about access to food, oil and other raw materials; America worries about the Japanese threat to its high-tech industries. The Wisemen's Commission could be charged with drawing up plans for a "mutual economic security treaty" between the United States and Japan. In such a treaty, Japan would be guaranteed access to American (including Alaskan) oil, food and raw materials. The United States would be guaranteed access to Japan's leading-edge technologies and markets through licensing, direct investment, joint enterprises and a variety of other means. If such a treaty could provide freedom from anxieties and paranoia, the entire relationship could move away from the prevailing acrimony toward closer collaboration.

If all this sounds visionary and difficult to implement, consider the alternative. The U.S. bilateral deficit with Japan would continue to grow, leading to further calls for protectionist legislation. This, in turn, would lead to retaliation, recrimination and a search for different partnerships. Each side would seek to gain technological superiority in a zero-sum game. Industrial espionage would run rampant. Japan would turn toward markets and raw materials from the Chinese and Soviets. Japan would find it necessary to protect a widening economic sphere in Asia and the Pacific, placing it in direct confrontation with the United States and upsetting the balance of power.

No rational person would hope for such an outcome. But that is where we are headed today in the absence of a serious decision by leaders on both sides to change course. The scheme above is ambitious and unprecedented, but so are the size and interdependence of our two economies. No lesser goal can be worthy of the two leading democracies of the world than to resolve their differences and discharge the responsibilities toward the entire planet which greatness has thrust upon them. They must face together the problem of their mutual success—lest they be destroyed by it.

THE U.S. AND JAPAN: SHARING OUR DESTINIES[10]

The most important bilateral relationship in the world today is that between the United States and Japan. It was only 44 years ago that our two countries were at war. In the short span of time since 1945 we have constructed an enormously complex relationship that touches all aspects of both societies and much of international human endeavor. The victor and vanquished of World War II have become the cornerstones of the international economic system, together producing almost 40 percent of the world's GNP. That all this has been accomplished in only four decades helps to explain why we find that there are still details to work out in managing this critical relationship.

This relationship is of immense benefit to the peoples of both nations. The United States enjoys the support of a strong, loyal and democratic ally in the Pacific, which contributes greatly to regional peace and prosperity. Japan has the protection of the U.S. nuclear umbrella and enjoys great access to the U.S. market, the world's largest. The two countries' foreign policies and foreign aid programs complement and support each other. Our individual and cooperative scientific and technological achievements have brought about a new age of information, increased our knowledge of ourselves and of our world, and contributed to the welfare of all nations. The lives of both peoples are enriched by a vast and burgeoning network of educational and cultural exchanges.

The sum, two nations that historically have acted quite independently have become interdependent. Neither nation can sur-

[10]Reprint of an article by Mike Mansfield, former U.S. Senator, and U.S. Ambassador to Japan, 1979–1989. Reprinted by permission of *Foreign Affairs*, Spring 1989. Copyright © 1989 by the Council on Foreign Relations, Inc.

vive at the current level of economic welfare and security without the active cooperation of the other.

This fundamental aspect of our relationship has been overshadowed in the media and in our bilateral dialogue by a seemingly endless series of disputes over market access and unfair trade practices. At times these frictions have spilled over and threatened to damage other areas of our economic partnership as well as our political, security and diplomatic cooperation.

I do not for a minute deny the importance of, and the need for, a fair and effective resolution of trade problems between the United States and Japan. But these frictions must be addressed in the context of an overall partnership that embraces all aspects of our relationship.

It was in March 1977 that I received a phone call from President Jimmy Carter that began a new life for my wife Maureen and me in Japan, after a full career in public service. Last December, after eleven-and-a-half years as U.S. ambassador in Tokyo, I left Japan to return to retirement. When we departed, both my wife and I were convinced that the individual destinies of Japan and America form a common structure vital to the future of both, as well as the rest of the world.

Let us examine the substance of this partnership.

II

Japan's postwar development owes much to the international free trade system, a system sustained primarily by the willingness of the United States to keep its market open, even at the cost of substantial dislocation in important U.S. industries such as steel and automobiles. The United States did not do this to be altruistic but rather out of the conviction that its economy would be strengthened through free trade and the laws of comparative advantage. Free trade has had and continues to have enormous benefits for the U.S. economy, but for too long Japan did not bear its fair share of the burden of maintaining the system by paying the short-term domestic political and economic costs of opening its own markets to foreign goods.

This is changing. In 1986 Japan established a framework for a major restructuring of its economic, prompted by altered exchange rates. It reduced the role of exports in stimulating economic growth by increasing domestic demand, thereby expanding manufactured imports and helping Japan to share the global economic burden. This has occurred at considerable political costs, resulting in some minor social and economic dislocations in Japan. But on the whole I believe that the Japanese economy and people have benefited.

Japan still has a considerable distance to go before its markets are as open as those of the United States, but the combination of the restructuring of Japan's economy, U.S. success in individual negotiations and the upward reevaluation of the yen are resulting in dramatic changes in the right direction.

Let us examine in detail the progress to date. In the last two years Japan's external sector was actually a drag on GNP growth. Instead, it was rapidly expanding domestic demand—up 5.1 percent—which boosted Japan's GNP growth rate to 4.3 percent in 1987 and an estimated six percent in 1988. The trade numbers also reflect this fundamental change. Imports to Japan, largely a function of domestic demand, are expected to be up roughly 28 percent this year, compared to a 16-percent increase in exports. Also, the prospects are good for about a seven-percent decline in Japan's current account surplus in 1988. The ratio of manufactured imports to Japan's total imports has increased from 31 percent in 1985 to 50 percent recently. Moreover, the U.S.-Japanese bilateral trade imbalance has been improving. The deficit dropped to $55.4 billion in 1988 from $59.8 billion the previous year. Particularly impressive has been the surge in U.S. exports to Japan—up 34 percent in 1988 to $37.7 billion. Although monthly trade numbers will continue to fluctuate, these figures indicate that we are headed toward a healthier balance of trade.

Progress on the serious issue of market access has also been impressive. Japan, on the prodding of the United States and other trading partners, has opened up to a significant extent its telcommunications, tobacco and pharmaceuticals markets, and reduced its tariffs to among the lowest in the world. In 1988 Japan acceded to the decision of a General Agreement on Tariffs and Trade panel, agreeing to allow freer trade in some categories of food products. Agreements providing for access to public works, and to beef and citrus markets, were also concluded. These market-opening measures are significant for the increased sales they will provide to U.S. suppliers—U.S. exports in these sectors are expected to increase by billions of dollars over the next few years—and also because they are concrete evidence of

Japan's commitment to trade liberalization. Rice poses a special problem that both governments have agreed should be addressed on a multilateral basis in the Uruguay Round of GATT.

INVESTMENT

At the end of 1987 the United States had direct holdings in Japan worth $14.3 billion, making the United States Japan's largest foreign investor. There are only five countries in the world that host more American investment: Canada ($57 billion), the United Kingdom ($45 billion), Germany ($24 billion), Switzerland ($20 billion) and Bermuda ($18 billion). Moreover, the average annual return on American direct investment in Japan over the last five years has been a striking 21 percent—more than U.S. investment in any other region and, in my opinion, solid evidence of the rewards that can be reaped by American firms that commit themselves to establishing operations in the Japanese market. Start-up has not been easy by any stretch of the imagination, or cheap, but it is clear that the rewards are well worth it.

Japan at the end of 1987 had direct investments worth $33 billion in the United States, much of them due to the recent increase in value of the yen. Media attention regarding Japanese investments has triggered a debate in some quarters of the United States. What has not been mentioned in this debate is the fact that the $33 billion in Japanese investment is far less than the $75 billion in British investment and the $47 billion in investment by the Netherlands. I welcome Japanese investment, as do the 47 U.S. state governors who came to Japan during my tenure to seek new jobs, new capital sources, new tax contributions and development opportunities.

Investment benefits both countries. Japanese direct investment in the United States creates jobs, expands the tax base, provides healthy competition for American firms on their home turf, and often brings new technology and innovative management techniques into the U.S. economy. Japanese portfolio investment in the United States, which totals $160 billion, helps to finance the U.S. fiscal deficit and to keep interest rates from rising, while it provides Japan with a safe and profitable haven for excess capital.

SCIENCE AND TECHNOLOGY

Japan's postwar development has been greatly assisted by access to U.S. technology through the traditional openness of the American scientific community, by study and research opportunities at American university research centers, and through licensing arrangements with U.S. firms. The flow of researchers and technical information has been generally one-way, but recently both governments have taken steps to increase U.S. access to Japan's scientific community through a new science and technology agreement. The Japanese government has also initiated a program to invite more than 200 American researchers for placement in Japanese research facilities. There are still some structural problems to be addressed. Research in the United States is based largely in universities, while in Japan it is largely based in industries. And we must confront the fact that few U.S. scientists and technicians are prepared to do research in the Japanese language. But here, too, we are moving in the right direction.

III

For all that the United States and Japan have achieved, both sides need to do more to achieve a better balance in their economic relationship. Japan must take further steps in its initiatives to remove impediments that hinder foreigners from doing business there or enjoying access to Japanese research and technology. It cannot afford to wait until foreign pressure builds up and a confrontation results. The Japanese government has already done much at the macroeconomic level to stimulate domestic demand and thus imports. The United States has also been successful in sectoral negotiations on such items as wood products, medical equipment, telecommunications, beef and citrus. Remaining barriers relate primarily to difficult, socially embedded areas such as Japan's labyrinthine distribution system, strong supplier-customer bonds and Japanese suspicions of the quality, safety and "after-service" associated with foreign products.

But old habits are crumbling under the impact of the high yen, with discount houses specializing in low-cost imports springing up all over Japan. Japan's leaders should work to continue removing these barriers until not a trace remains to support allegations of a closed Japanese market.

The United States, however, faces the greater challenge. As a nation we have become soft. We have allowed the technology and manufacturing base of our industries to languish, and we have neglected quality and service. This has allowed Japanese firms and others to capture much of our market. The emphasis in American industry has been on short-term profits rather than long-term market growth. This is the reverse of the Japanese approach. Thus, when the upward yen reevaluation created opportunities for U.S. manufacturers to gain back their markets at home and abroad, many companies took this opening to raise prices once again—a terrible waste of opportunity.

The United States must also confront its national budget deficit and its $140-billion global trade deficit, not only its $54-billion deficit with Japan. In an unsettlingly short time, the United States has gone from the world's greatest creditor nation to the world's biggest debtor.

Americans need to save more (the average Japanese saves 19 percent of the family take-home pay), produce more and consume less. Our primary and secondary education system desperately needs reform if we are going to produce young people able to compete technologically in the world. Higher education must be made affordable to all Americans who have the requisite ability and desire. We must use our technological capability to improve our own production system. And we must reduce our dependence on short-term profits and look instead toward long-term business and industrial strategies.

As the United States and Japan undertake these individual economic responsibilities it is equally important to reduce the rhetoric and political heat each directs toward the other. The United States, in particular, needs to find a less contentious mechanism to handle trade problems. There have been a number of suggestions along this line. Some have proposed the establishment of a bilateral businessmen's council that would take up trade disputes before they become issues in U.S. trade law or in GATT. I have also suggested that the United States should look at some variations of a free trade agreeement to see if there are not ways of applying this approach to trade negotiations with Japan. As our two countries become more interdependent, friction will likely increase even further in areas of trade and the economy. We must therefore find a better way to address these disturbances.

DEFENSE

Perhaps no other aspect of the U.S.-Japanese relationship is misunderstood as frequently as our security relations. What ought to be a source of pride for both nations as a brilliant achievement of international cooperation is sometimes dismissed as a "free ride" for the Japanese. Let us take a closer look.

Much of the debate focuses on Japan's defense spending. Some argue that Japan spends too little, yet the one percent of GNP that it spends on defense amounts to $30 billion. This is comparable to the $35 billion spent by the United Kingdom, the $32 billion spent by France and the $31 billion spent by the Federal Republic of Germany. Moreover, if one includes the additional $10-billon worth of pensions and survivors' benefits, which the Japanese handle in a separate budget (unlike the United States and European nations), Japan's defense spending considerably exceeds the expenditures of our European allies.

Japan uses this spending for the mutually agreed objectives of maintaining a defense capability to protect its home islands and two sea-lanes out to 1,000 miles, the first extending from the Bay of Tokyo southeast to the region of Guam, and the second from Osaka Bay southwest to the Bashi Channel.

This "small" defense budget buys Japan more destroyers and more antisubmarine aircraft than the United States deploys in the Western Pacific and more F-15s than the United States has for defending its homeland. The Japanese commitment to the joint development of the FSX fighter, to the production under license of 100 P3C antisubmarine aircraft, and to the purchase of such advanced warning systems as the Aegis ensures that its defense capability will be the best possible, that it will be compatible with American defense systems and that it will be developed in cooperation with U.S. defense industries.

This joint defense effort pays enormous dividends to both countries. The United States will defend Japan if the need ever arises. By the same token, the increased capabilities of Japan's own defense forces have allowed the United States to stretch its resources to other parts of the immense Pacific Basin area.

In addition to increasingly carrying the burden of its own defense, the Japanese government provides direct financial support for the upkeep of the 63,000 American military personnel stationed in the archipelago, military forces that play a vital role not only in Japan's defense but in the defense of the region as a whole. Japan currently contributes $2.7 billion of the total cost of $6.2 billion to keep these American forces in Japan. This amounts to about 40 percent of the total cost, or $45,000 per military person—the most generous support provided by any ally. This financial support, moreover, will increase in the years to come.

Joint weapons development projects such as the FSX aircraft program, which has been the subject of debate in the U.S. government, have much promise for the future. They ensure compatibility of U.S. and Japanese weapons systems. They assure participation in very large projects by U.S. industry and access to Japanese technological developments. And they assure that Japan and the United States continue to work together in providing for the defense of Japan and Asia. Some have argued that such programs transfer technology to Japan's defense industry, which at some future date might become a competitor to the U.S. defense industry. While there is some risk in this, Japan does not permit the export of military equipment at the present time and, in my view, is not likely to do so. Thus, it is far better to be a player and a partner with Japan than to force Japan to go it alone and develop an indigenous technology that would, indeed, compete with the United States.

When I was in Tokyo, I heard two sorts of complaints from visiting Americans about Japan's defense policy. The "free ride" group argued that the time had come for Japan to shake off its postwar constraints on defense and to take on regional responsibilities that the United States could no longer afford and which were dragging down our economy. A smaller group argued that there was a new nationalism awakening in Japan that would lead it toward becoming an independent military power and that the United States should therefore be wary of Japan's increasing military capability.

While there has always been a very tiny but vociferous minority in Japan in favor of an offensively armed Japan, such opinions have never been more than a media curiosity. The new Japanese generation is more confident. This is to be expected and is welcome. I remember a postwar America that tended to be rather cocksure that it was the center of the world stage. Perhaps this kind of self-assuredness is necessary for a new economic superpower to assume its legitimate role in world affairs. But this confidence should not be confused with a desire for a strong military role for Japan. The Japanese people remain strongly pacifistic and their attitudes have little in common with the prewar generation. Not only is war truly abhorrent to them; they are also perfectly aware that there are far better, humane and effective ways of pursuing legitimate international goals. They also realize that their Asian neighbors do not want a remilitarized Japan. Nor does the United States.

As we look at the many tangible benefits the United States derives from this fruitful security relationship, we should count our blessings to have as a close and loyal ally the strongest, most stable democracy and greatest economic superpower in the region. We need to remember that the U.S. forces in Japan are stationed there in America's interest as much as in Japan's. At a time when U.S. bases in other parts of Asia are under pressure, we must ask ourselves: If the United States were to lose its bases in Japan, where would we draw our new defense perimeter? How much would it cost to establish that new defense perimeter? And how could the United States maintain its strategic influence in the most dynamic region in the world?

In sum, the long-term benefits of the defense relationship must not be put at risk by shortsighted and ill-conceived demands for a greatly enhanced Japanese defense effort. Japan should and will do more to support joint defense efforts, but we must recognize what is already being done, how much the United States benefits from this relationship, and how much the United States will lose if cooperation is replaced by confrontation.

IV

Cooperation between the United States and Japan, as the two largest economic powers in the world and as two important democracies, is essential to address development and political problems around the world. I do not mean to imply a U.S.-Japanese "condominium" in Asia or elsewhere, but these two countries by virtue of their economic strength will have to take a leading role along with like-minded states in creating and maintaining the kind of international environment that benefits everyone. Our current cooperation on trade in the Uruguay Round of GATT and on debt relief are examples. This aspect of the relationship is just beginning to be developed, but I believe that as the United

States and Japan move into the next decade, global political and economic cooperation will replace bilateral trade confrontation as the watchword of the relationship.

Foreign economic assistance is one area for such cooperation. The United States has traditionally borne the greatest foreign assistance burden through its aid program and by keeping its market open to the agricultural and industrial products from the developing world, and it must continue to play a major role in this area. The United States must also acknowledge, however, that Japan's aid program will soon become the largest in the world. Japan already surpasses the United States in terms of the ratio of overseas development assistance to GNP (0.23 percent for the United States versus 0.31 percent for Japan) and aid per capita (the United States spends annually $39.60 per American and Japan spends $46.40 per Japanese citizen).

In 1988 Japan appropriated a total of $10.4 billion for economic assistance. Aware of the need to recyle its trade surpluses to the most needy nations, Japan pledged at the seven-nation summit in Montreal concessional flows totaling at least $50 billion over the next five years. It also promised to improve the "quality" of its aid by increasing the percentage of grants and untied assistance. Specifically, it announced that by 1990 all of its aid to the Philippines, Thailand and Malaysia will be completely untied. The United States can expect that this policy will be extended to loans to other countries as well.

Geographically, Japan's overseas development assistance remains strongly oriented toward the Asian Pacific region. There are obvious historical and political reasons for this orientation. Its assistance has been effective; the stable and prosperous environment in East Asia since 1975 owes much to Japanese aid and trade. But Japan is also currently one of the top benefactors of Pakistan, Turkey and Egypt, and has begun increasing assistance to Mexico, South and Central America, the Caribbean and sub-Saharan Africa. Japan recently indicated that it was prepared to provide substantial financial support for the return of refugees to Afghanistan—and to support peacekeeping forces—after the pullout of Soviet troops. And it has offered to do the same in Cambodia and elsewhere.

It is fortunate that Japan's foreign policy interests coincide almost completely with those of the United States; the recipients that the Japanese government selects for such aid are generally those countries that the United States would like to see receive support. Since the U.S. aid budget is unlikely to increase in the near future and because so much of its aid is "earmarked" for special countries such as Israel and Egypt, Japan can play a critical role in promoting economic development and political stability in regions that are important to the United States and the West as a whole.

Japan is also making a significant contribution in absorbing an increasing share of manufactured products from developing countries. Japan has increased its imports from Asia's newly industrialized economies by over 70 percent in the last two years, albeit from a very low level. Almost all of this represents manufactured goods such as textiles and electronics, making Japan an engine of growth for the region.

None of these developments should be regarded as an excuse for the United States to reduce its aid program further; diminishing aid means diminishing influence, and this is not in the U.S. interest, nor as the Japanese remind us, in the interest of Japan. But, in assessing our partnership, Japan's role in our mutual effort to promote economic security, well-being and development for less fortunate regions of the world deserves U.S. attention and acknowledgment.

Global cooperation between the United States and Japan extends beyond economic assistance. In the United Nations, the United States and Japan work as closely as any two allies in pursuit of shared interests. On regional issues, including Afghanistan, Cambodia, the Middle East and even Central America, Japan is an increasingly active player and contributor. Indeed, it could be argued that there is greater harmony between the United States and Japan on foreign policy issues than with any other country. In the years ahead Japan may take an active role in international peacekeeping activities and in finding other areas to contribute politically. I do not mean to suggest that a more active Japanese foreign policy will always produce initiatives to our liking, but as I noted, we share the same fundamental interests and objectives—a more secure, democratic and prosperous world.

V

A little over a year ago, some congressional representatives, to protest the selling by Toshiba Machine Company of high-technology equipment to the Soviet Union, took a sledgehammer to an audiotape player manufactured by a different Toshiba subsidiary. The photos of this event were printed much more widely in Japan than in the United States, and the picture remains etched clearly in the minds of many Japanese as an example of American contempt for Japan.

A new phrase was added to the Japanese language in the aftermath of this event, *Nihon Tataki*—Japan-bashing. The legitimate U.S. concern over the sale of vital defense-related technology to the Soviets by an ally was lost to the Japanese public in all this emotion. For their part, Americans ignored the stiff penalties meted out by the Japanese government to the Toshiba Machine executives involved, the resignation of the chief executive officer of the parent Toshiba Corporation (which was not involved in the sale), and the immediate steps taken by the Japanese government to tighten up the enforcement of regulations by the Coordination Committee for Multilateral Export Controls and to increase penalties for violators.

As a result, the facts were lost and events were distorted beyond recognition, but the images and the anger remain. It is not surprising, in countries that have proceeded from sworn enemies to close partners in little more than 40 years, that people occasionally allow emotion to overshadow reason. But I am concerned that emotional responses will erode the goodwill in both Japan and the United States. Self-restraint is needed on both sides. We know a great deal about each other, but we do not always understand.

This gap in understanding is narrowing. Fortunately, as healthy democracies we have a rich fabric of exchanges. The flow of travelers from Japan to the United States exceeded two-and-a-half million last year. The flow in the other direction was smaller but still significant. Future travelers will find their trips made a bit easier because our two governments just recently put in place a system of waivers so that tourists will no longer be bothered with the necessity of seeking visas to travel between the two countries for short stays.

Last year at least 20,000 Japanese came to the United States to attend high school or college. The number of high school exchange students would have been larger but there are simply not enough host families available in the United States to accommodate Japanese youngsters wanting to attend an American school.

In part because of the high value of the yen and language difficulties, the number of Americans studying in Japan is much fewer, under 2,000. Nevertheless, I am pleased to note that in 1986 over 23,400 U.S. college students were enrolled in Japanese-language courses and that nearly 100 American high schools teach Japanese. This is a significant step. It exposes children at an early age to a country that will be an important part of their future.

The Japanese government has also begun an innovative and exciting program that is now in its third year. It is called the Japan Exchange and English Teaching Program. Under this initiative, 3,000 college graduates from a number of English-speaking countries (the bulk of them from the United States) spend a year in Japanese high schools or prefectural offices serving as English-language resource persons and advisers on international projects.

There are also many joint university projects, centers and faculty exchanges under way. A very recent phenomenon has been the establishment of some 12 branch campuses of American colleges operating in Japan with half a dozen more in the offing. These campuses have a fine potential for contributing to educational exchange and greater understanding between young Americans and Japanese.

Many traditional programs that have for years contributed to our mutual cultural understanding now grow more important in this age of interdependence. The U.S.-Japan Conference on Cultural and Educational Interchange conducts a periodic evaluation of our cultural relationship and focuses both countries' attention on those areas which need help. The Japan-U.S. Educational (Fulbright) Commission continues to play a key role in the intellectual exchange between the two nations, as it has for 40 years.

VI

More than anything else, this is what the past eleven years or so have meant: establishing one friendship at a time, treating others as we would have them treat us, arguing when necessary and doing so with firmness and without equivocation, but always keeping in mind that we are speaking with friends—the best friends the United States has in that part of the world.

What we have been able to achieve in these years will be for others to judge, but we leave with our heads held high and our arms swinging. The relationship is sound. In most areas the relationship is exemplary, notably in the areas of security, foreign policy cooperation, foreign aid and cultural exchange, among others. In trade, we still have much to learn, but we can build on our recent successes, and we will find that a better mechanism exists for keeping our disagreements from being blown out of proportion. I am optimistic because neither the United States nor Japan has the option of going it alone anymore. The ocean that divided us now unites us. Every year more and more individuals on both sides of the Pacific understand the importance of and are working for the betterment of the U.S.-Japanese partnership— the most important relationship in the world, bar none.

BIBLIOGRAPHY

An asterisk (*) preceding a reference indicates that the article or part of it has been reprinted in this book.

BOOKS AND PAMPHLETS

Abegglen, James C. The strategy of Japanese business. Ballinger. '84.

Alston, Jon P. The American samurai: blending American and Japanese managerial practices. W. de Gruyter. '85.

Boyd, Gavin. Pacific trade, investment, and politics. St. Martin's Press. '89.

Burstein, Daniel. Japan's new financial empire and its threat to America. Simon & Schuster. '88.

Cohen, Stephen D. Uneasy partnership: competition and conflict in U.S.-Japanese trade relations. Ballinger. '85.

Davidson, William. The amazing race: winning the technorivalry with Japan. Wiley. '84.

Duke, Benjamin C. The Japanese school: lessons for industrial America. Praeger. '86.

El-Agraa, Ali M. Japan's trade frictions. St. Martin's Press. '88.

Frantz, Douglas and Collins, Catherine. Selling out: how we are letting Japan buy our land, our industries, our financial institutions, and our future. Contemporary Books. '89.

Frost, Ellen L. For richer, for poorer: the new U.S.-Japan relationship. Council on Foreign Relations. '87.

Gibney, Frank. Miracle by design: the real reasons behind Japan's economic success. Times Books. '82.

Graham, John and Sano, Yoshihiro. Smart bargaining; doing business with Japan. Ballinger. '84.

Hall, Edward and Mildred. Hidden differences: doing business with Japan. Doubleday. '87.

Hayashi, Kichiro. The U.S.-Japanese economic relationship: can it be improved? New York University Press. '89.

Iriye, Akira and Cohen, Warren. The United States and Japan in the postwar world. University of Kentucky Press. '89.

Lauren, Paul and Wylie, Raymond. Destinies shared: the U.S.-Japanese relations. Westview Press. '89.

Laxer, James. Decline of the superpowers: winners and losers in today's global economy. Paragon House. '89.

Lewis, Hunter and Allison, Donald. The real world war: the coming battle for the new global economy and why we are in danger of losing. Coward, McCann & Geoghegan. '82.

Malerba, Franco. The semiconductor business: the economics of rapid growth and decline. University of Wisconsin Press. '85.

McCraw, Thomas K. America versus Japan. Harvard Business School Press. '86.

Mehtabdin, Khalid R. Comparative management: business styles in Japan and the United States. E. Mellen Press. '86.

Metraux, Daniel A. The Japanese economy in transition and the United States. E. Mellen Press. '89.

Morishima, Michio. Why has Japan 'succeeded'? Cambridge University Press. '82.

Peterson, Lorna. U.S.-Japanese Competition: A Bibliography. Vance Bibliographies. '89.

Prestowitz, Clyde V. Trading places: how we allowed Japan to take the lead. Basic Books. '88.

Sobel, Robert. IBM vs. Japan: the struggle for the future. Stein and Day. '86.

Striner, Herbert E. Regaining the lead: policies for economic growth. Praeger. '84.

Turner, Louis. Industrial collaboration with Japan. Routledge & Kegan Paul. '87.

Vogel, Ezra. Comeback, case by case: building the resurgence of American business. Simon & Schuster. '85.

Vogel, Ezra. Japan as number one: lessons for America. Harper & Row. '85.

Wachtel, Paul. Trade friction and economic policy; problems and prospects for Japan and the United States. Cambridge University Press. '87.

ADDITIONAL PERIODICAL ARTICLES WITH ABSTRACTS

For those who wish to read more widely on the subject of Japan and the U.S., this section contains abstracts of additional articles that bear on the topic. Readers who require a comprehensive list of materials are advised to consult the *Readers' Guide to Periodical Literature* and other Wilson indexes.

Let them defend themselves. James M. Fallows *The Atlantic* 263:17–18+ Ap '89

Many Americans wrongly believe that the solution to the trade problems between America and Japan is to stop giving Japan a free ride on defense. Because of the memories Asians have of World War II, prodding Japan to expand its military would be extremely unpopular in Japan and elsewhere in Asia. Moreover, given the defense burdens that Japan has already assumed, it is difficult to see what it could spend a lot of extra money on. Forcing Japan to pay for more of America's military costs is not an option either. America needs Japan's cooperation at least as much as Japan needs U.S. protection, and Japan already bears much of the cost of American troops stationed on its territory. The military relationship between Japan and America, while not perfect, is better than any of the alternatives that have been suggested. The trade problems are a separate matter and should be dealt with accordingly.

U.S. falling behind Japan in superconductor research. Bruce D. Nordwall *Aviation Week & Space Technology* 130:57+ Ja 16 '89

A Defense Science Board report warns that the United States will be forced to rely on foreign sources for superconducting materials unless funding for research and development is drastically increased. Noting that such dependence on foreign sources is unacceptable to U.S. interests, the report recommends that the Pentagon increase funding for 1989 by 50 percent to $120 million and spend $245 million in 1992. Foreign investment in superconductivity far outstrips that of the United States, and Japan alone spends more than U.S. commercial and government efforts combined. To regain the lead, the United States must direct intensive research into the theory of high-temperature superconductors and into technology for fabricating thin films. The report concludes that superconductors could provide several new capabilities for the military, and many of these applications could also be of high value to scientific and business interests.

Can Japan keep its economy from hollowing out? Amy Borrus *Business Week* 52–5 Jl 13 '87

Part of a cover story on Japan's transformation into a world economic leader. The Japanese are working to avoid the mistakes that the United States made during the transition from a manufacturing-dominated economy to a service-oriented economy. Manufacturing will account for only 22 percent of Japan's employment by 1995, but civilian R&D expenditure is much higher than in the United States, and the trend to move operations overseas is unlikely to go as far in Japan as it has in America. Even so, basic industries will shrink drastically, and the auto and electronics industries will undergo shakeouts. Some companies in these industries are diversifying into services like fast food and bookselling to provide jobs for workers no longer needed in industry. Financial services, communications, health care, and business services will provide new white-collar employment. By 1995 nearly half of all jobs will be in the service sector, and economic growth could be weak.

Japan's no-trespassing sign is still up for U.S. contractors (public works projects). Steven J. Dryden *Business Week* 52–3 Mr 21 '88

The Japanese are planning to spend $200 billion on public works projects over the next ten years but are allowing U.S. firms to participate only in labor-intensive work. American retaliation may be forthcoming: the cabinet-level Economic Policy Council will decide whether to initiate a formal trade action, which could lead to tariffs. Congress, frustrated with the administration's inaction thus far, has already blocked Japanese access to federally funded public works projects in the United States. The government cannot block private Japanese construction projects in the U.S., but it could impose higher tariffs on goods or equipment imported for those projects. It could also impose penalties on Japanese companies that export construction equipment to the United States. Japanese prime minister Noboru Takeshita has promised a more flexible construction market, but he faces the challenge of forcing concessions from Japan's powerful construction lobby.

American food companies look yummy to Japan. Barbara Buell *Business Week* 61–2 Je 20 '88

As Japan begins to lower its barriers to cheap food imports, Japanese companies are moving to head off potential U.S. competitors by entering the American food industry. Japanese firms are taking advantage of the strong yen, establishing U.S. production bases for a range of food products. While Japanese trading companies have shipped agricultural products from the United States to Japan for some time, the current move is toward the higher-margin businesses of food processing, transportation, and distribution. The Japanese are signing contracts with U.S. manufacturers, lining up joint ventures, and looking to purchase U.S. food and beverage processors. The Japanese plan to export their products back to Japan but are likely to go after a piece of the U.S. market as well. The opening of the Japanese food market could take another two to four years, and U.S. experts are concerned that American companies will fall behind Japanese-owned processors.

On the campus: fat endowments and growing clout (Japanese endowments to U.S. universities). Leslie Helm *Business Week* 70+ Jl 11 '88

Part of a cover story on Japan's growing influence in the United States. Japanese corporations, which have given multimillion dollar grants to universities across the United States, have emerged as the largest foreign source of university research funding. The donations, which include an estimated $30 million in research contracts, are a modest investment designed to gain access to America's top minds. According to Chalmers Johnson, professor of international relations at the University of California at San Diego, some of the money is used to buy research that the Japanese can't get otherwise. By giving money to think tanks and universities, Japan may also be thwarting research that is critical of its economic practices. Universities and think tanks bristle at the latter suggestion but Japanese money may have more power than universities realize. An estimated 80 percent of the money being used for research on Japan, for example, now comes from Japanese sources.

Japan buys into the American dream (property investments).
Stewart Toy and Ted Holden *Business Week* 42 N 7 '88

The yen's rise against the dollar has led to a surge in Japanese investment in U.S. real estate. Leading the way is Japanese billionaire Genshiro Kawamoto, whose Marugen realty firm had invested $173 million in Hawaiian rental properties by last spring and is aiming to invest $500 million to build homes in California. Kawamoto recently bought land in Santa Rosa for 245 single-family houses, and he has already commenced construction of 350 homes near Sacramento. Other big Japanese realty firms and Japanese families have also become interested in American property. Not just the wealthy have entered the game; according to one Japanese realtor, most of his customers who invest in U.S. real estate earn less than $64,000 a year. Some observers warn that the buying spree could inspire widespread anti-Japanese sentiment.

When you can't beat 'em (Japanese real estate investors hiring American managers to run their U.S. properties). Ellen Paris
Forbes 141:52 My 16 '88

Some American real estate developers, facing office vacancy rates of between 13 and 22 percent, have stopped building and started managing buildings owned by the Japanese. According to one source, the Japanese will spend about $15 billion on American real estate in 1988, so it is likely that more management contracts will become available. Some other developers are taking advantage of Japanese real estate investment in the United States by building office space for Japanese owners on a fee basis.

The peril of pushing Japan. Joel Dreyfuss *Fortune* 115:113–14+
My 11 '87

Both Japan and the United States would suffer if a trade war were to result from the recently imposed U.S. tariffs on Japanese electronics. A vicious round of quotas, tariffs, and protectionist legislation in the United States and Japan would batter the U.S. economy with inflation and higher interest rates and increase unemployment in Japan. Furthermore, the U.S. computer industry would suffer from a shortage of Japanese computer chips, and U.S. farmers, already suffering a recession, would lose another major market. Recognizing that they stand to lose their largest market if they fall into a trade war, the Japanese have not retaliated for the recent U.S. tariffs.

America's competitive revival. Sylvia Nasar *Fortune* 117:44–50+
Ja 4 '88

Thanks in part to a cheaper dollar, many American industries have become the world's low-cost producers. American manufacturers did not
rely solely on a declining dollar to regain their competitive edge, however. A painful program of industrial modernization that included forceful
efforts to raise efficiency, slash costs, produce higher-quality goods, and
market products more aggressively preceded the resurgence of U.S. industry. In many industries, Japan and European countries lost their price
advantage as their currencies became strong against the dollar and their
labor costs increased. While enhanced competitiveness will allow the
United States to recapture some of its former influence in the world's
markets, the nation cannot expect to regain the economic preeminence
of its post–World War II years. Competition from its major trading partners and from newly industrializing countries in Latin America and East
Asia will limit U.S. gains.

Is Japan as rich as you think? Bill Powell *Newsweek* 109:48–50
Je 8 '87

Many Americans see Japan as a relentlessly productive society awash in
excess money, but the reality of everyday life for most middle-class Japanese citizens belies the country's impressive economic statistics. Aging
basic industries and a strong yen have slowed domestic spending, dampened export growth, and caused a massive outflow of Japanese currency.
An outdated tax system geared to an agrarian Japan that no longer exists
has taken thousands of desperately needed acres out of the commercial
and housing market and driven real estate prices sky-high. Last week
Prime Minister Yasuhiro Nakasone unveiled a dramatic expansionary
budget policy to stimulate domestic spending. If Japan's economy is not
reformed soon, Nakasone and his party will risk a trade war abroad and
rising political discontent at home. Three affluent Japanese are profiled.

The salarymen blues (Japanese managers in the U.S.). John
Schwartz *Newsweek* 111:51–2 My 9 '88

With the increase in Japanese direct investment in the United States, the
number of Japanese executives relocating to America is growing. Japanese companies are finding it hard to fill overseas jobs, however, because
salarymen (midlevel Japanese executives) face immense difficulties in the
United States. On the job, Japanese executives are often quietly frustrated with American workers. At home, they worry that their American-
educated children will not get into Japan's top universities and often see
their wives leading lonely lives. Many Japanese expatriates cling to Japanese culture. In the New York area, Japanese television programs, news-
papers, and country clubs cater to 60,000 Japanese. In small towns,
however, employees and their families are encouraged to assimilate. Most
salarymen return home, but that also proves difficult: they are often treated as strangers and their children may suffer abuse in school as foreign-

ers.

The cop and the benefactor (U.S. and Japan). Russell Watson
Newsweek 113:36+ F 6 '89

Now that it is on the verge of surpassing the United States as the world's
leading donor of foreign aid, Japan has been receiving high praise from
the Bush administration for its generosity. Others, however, are concerned that Japan is using foreign aid to gain political and commercial advantages over the United States in several geopolitical areas. There is a
danger that Japan will become the world's primary benefactor while the
United States will be relegated to the role of the world's policeman. As
a result, some officials in Washington want Japan to share more of the security burden. Japan already spends a great deal on defense, however,
and neither the United States nor Japan's neighbors want Japan to become a military superpower again. The United States is therefore trying
to convince Japan to change its methods of dispensing foreign aid. Japanese aid has often been tied to commercial interests and made as repay-
able development loans rather than outright grants.

Next stop, Tinseltown (investments in U.S. films). Joshua Ham-
mer *Newsweek* 113:48–9 Mr 20 '89

Japanese companies are entering the U.S. film industry. About a dozen
Tokyo-based firms have established film divisions since 1987. The Japanese have backed major projects and top producers and have even set
up a small studio, Apricot Entertainment. They have targeted the movie
business because of their desire to provide programs for the new generation of high definition television sets and because of their conviction that
a handful of giant global firms will eventually dominate the communications industry. The Japanese have shown some hesitancy, owing partly to
ill-fated past involvements in Hollywood and the difference in corporate
cultures between that city and conservative Tokyo. Nevertheless, at least
one major studio is likely to be bought by the Japanese in the next few
years, perhaps by electronics giant Sony.

The Rising Sun on U.S. real estate (Japanese investment).
Technology Review 90:80 Ag/S '87

According to a report by Russell C. Lindner and Edward L. Monahan, Jr.,
published by the MIT Center for Real Estate Development, Japanese real
estate activities in the United States are much more extensive than is generally thought. Most of the investments have been in large-scale office
buildings in areas that are known as centers of Japanese-American influence, such as San Francisco, Los Angeles, and Honolulu. Factors motivat-
ing such investments include favorable exchange rates, a shortage of
similar investment opportunities in Japan, and a weakening Japanese construction market. Lindner and Monahan believe that Japan's activities
will benefit the U.S. real estate business.

Eyes on the prize (significance of Japanese innovations as measured by patents issued in the U.S.). Barbara Rudolph *Time* 131:50-1 Mr 21 '88

According to a recent study of patents for the National Science Foundation, Japanese innovations may be more significant than those developed by Americans. Based on the assumption that the citation of a patent in other patent applications indicates its impact on subsequent research, the study showed that the Japanese are ahead of Americans in significant technological developments. Critics of the study contend that commercially valuable patents are not always frequently cited. Regardless of such criticism, the Japanese have built an impressive record in a broad range of industries. For the first time ever, the top three recipients of U.S. patents last year were Japanese. The Japanese edge is partly due to the focus in Japan on commercial products rather than on long-term military or scientific applications. In addition, Japanese goods are marketed more quickly than American products.

Japan's search for U.S. colleges (attempts to buy various colleges). Susan Tifft *Time* 133:57 Ja 23 '89

Japanese businessmen and educators are shopping for U.S. colleges, hoping to expand study-abroad opportunities for Japanese students. In recent months the Japanese have offered to bail out a number of financially ailing schools in exchange for control of their governing boards. No institutions have relinquished complete control, but a few have negotiated deals that allow them to retain independence. Meanwhile, several U.S. universities are expanding into Japan. Some educators are worried about the possibility of Japan buying U.S. schools, which they see as the ultimate technology transfer. On the other hand, the deals provide not only a source of revenue for U.S. institutions but also important links to Japanese business and a chance for American students and faculty to be exposed to Japanese culture.

How to beat the Japanese: five U.S. companies rise to the challenge (cover story; special section). Clemens P. Work, Mary Lord and Robert H. Bork Jr. *U.S. News & World Report* 103:38-45 Ag 24 '87

A special section on how U.S. companies can compete with the Japanese highlights five U.S. companies that are successfully doing so and one Japanese conglomerate, Mitsui, that is devising strategies for leapfrogging the Americans. Eastman Kodak, Goodyear Tire & Rubber, Texas Instruments, Morgan Stanley, and Brown-Forman have been successful because they have given American workers the knowledge and initiative to turn out quality products at low cost; adapted to rapid change; exercised patience and tenacity; adjusted to local practices; and paid adequate attention to marketing. Japanese firms have responded to the high yen by setting up factories in other countries like Brazil and Taiwan and by moving into new fields like biotechnology and office automation.

Zen and the art of cashing in (Americans learning to speak Japanese for business purposes). Jim Impoco *U.S. News & World Report* 104:40–1 Mr 28 '88

American businesses that operate in Japan are increasingly seeking employees who speak Japanese. Bilingual staffers reduce the costs associated with translators, enhance American firms' social access to Japanese executives, and bolster an American manager's authority and a company's morale. Some 23,454 Americans currently study Japanese at U.S. colleges, an increase of about 45 percent since 1984. Japanese firms have begun to employ bilingual foreigners as overseas branch staffers or in-house advisers.

The sun also prizes (Japanese gifts to American universities). Clemens P. Work *U.S. News & World Report* 105:45 Ag 15 '88

Computer titan Fujitsu has made a grant of $1.5 million to the Massachusetts Institute of Technology (MIT) to endow a chair in electrical engineering and computer science. The gift brings to 11, out of a total of 180, the number of permanent chairs at the university that are endowed by Japanese companies. The fear that Japan is purchasing undue influence at U.S. universities appears unfounded, however. According to a congressional study released in 1986, Japan is involved in less than 1 percent of American university R&D. Donors to MIT receive periodic access to professors but no advance looks at their research.

Has the Orient totally conquered U.S. electronics? Seven companies say no (cover story). Merrill C. Lehrer *USA Today* (Periodical) 117:16–22 Ja '89

Despite many observers' belief that America can no longer compete against the Japanese in the consumer electronics business, some U.S. electronics firms are thriving by offering world-class products. Seven successful U.S. consumer electronics companies are briefly discussed: Mobile Fidelity Sound Lab of Petaluma, California; Kash 'N Gold of Farmingdale, New York; Harman America of Woodbury, New York; Black & Decker of Towson, Maryland; Zenith Electronics Corporation of Glenview, Illinois; Roland Corporation of Los Angeles, California; and Smith Corona Corporation of New Canaan, Connecticut.